The Leader Connection

The Foundation

Michael T. Parker

Copyright 2025
ISBN 979-8-9991700-2-6

Printed in the USA

Dedication

In Honor of
Granddad"

Louis Bryant
April 5, 1912 – August 6, 1997

Table of Contents

Introduction

30-Year Reflection

The Heartbeat of Leadership Connection

Over thirty years of leading and growing with teams, I have come to see leadership as so much more than the pursuit of outcomes or the management of tasks—it is a living, breathing commitment to foster deep human connection and transformation. Early in my journey, I was driven by the desire to achieve, to move metrics, to deliver results. Yet, as the years unfolded, I began to understand that the real heart of leadership is igniting possibility within others and equipping everyone to discover and realize their own greatness. This revelation fundamentally altered my approach, guiding me away from seeing leadership as a position of power, and towards embracing it as a purpose rooted in service, openness, and the celebration of what makes each person unique.

The core lesson I carry is that true leadership is built upon authentic bonds that are grounded in unwavering values. A team's potential blooms not from control, but from cultivating a culture where trust, respect, and shared vision are ever-present. When leaders set the tone by honoring every voice and inviting every perspective into the fold, something extraordinary happens—a sense of unity and belonging emerges. The team's energy aligns, enthusiasm soars, and together, the group achieves more than they ever thought possible.

Empathy has become my guiding star throughout this journey. By seeing and honoring the wholeness of each person—their hopes, their struggles, their aspirations - we create a foundation of trust that deepens conversations and opens the door to courageous dialogue. Rallying people around a clear and inspiring vision transforms not only the work, but also the individuals themselves. When autonomy is granted and creativity is encouraged, innovation flourishes, and people feel empowered to stretch beyond boundaries.

The world is in constant flux, and adaptability is an essential skill for any leader who wishes to remain effective and inspiring. Humility has been my greatest teacher, showing me that learning never ends, and that reinvention is part of growth. Emotional intelligence has reshaped my journey, helping me navigate moments of chaos and uncertainty, and guiding me to model resilience, openness, and personal evolution for my teams.

Through adversity, I have witnessed the power of resilience and courage. Leadership is not about never falling; it is about rising, again and again, drawing wisdom from setbacks and maintaining authenticity even when the path is rocky. The storms I have weathered with my teams have only strengthened our bonds, inspiring us to persevere and build something meaningful together.

I have also learned that diversity and inclusion are not optional, but essential to a thriving team. The beauty and strength that emerge from different perspectives, backgrounds, and experiences cannot be overstated. When every person feels seen, valued, and heard, the collective potential of the team expands exponentially, and the environment becomes one of innovation and mutual support.

Recognition, appreciation, and integrity are the backbone of leadership that lasts. By acknowledging the unique contributions and achievements of everyone, we fuel both growth and loyalty. Integrity, meanwhile, ensures that our actions remain aligned with our values, anchoring us in authenticity and trust.

Ultimately, I have come to see leadership as a delicate balance—a dance of empathy, vision, adaptability, humility, resilience, and gratitude. It is a call to serve, to connect, to inspire, and to transform. When we lead with heart and conviction, we do more than guide teams; we change lives and shape legacies that reach far beyond ourselves.

1

Understanding The Role of Leadership in Employee Connection

In today's rapidly evolving workplace, the role of leadership has transformed significantly. Leaders are no longer seen merely as decision-makers or task managers; they are increasingly recognized as essential facilitators of employee connection and engagement. This overview explores the multifaceted role of leadership in fostering meaningful connections among employees, examining key themes such as communication, emotional intelligence, inclusivity, and organizational culture. By understanding how leaders can effectively bridge the gap between management and employees, organizations can cultivate a more engaged, motivated, and connected workforce.

However, it is crucial for leaders to be aware of their own leadership style and how it impacts their team. Different leadership styles can significantly influence the level of employee connection within an organization. If leaders are not mindful of their approach, they may inadvertently create barriers to engagement and connection. For instance, an autocratic leadership style may lead to quick decision-making but can also result in low morale and stifled creativity among team members. On the other hand, a transformational leadership style can inspire and motivate employees but may also set lofty expectations that can lead to stress and burnout.

By focusing not only on the needs of employees but also on understanding and adapting their own leadership style, leaders can create a positive and productive work environment. This chapter will delve into various leadership styles, highlighting the challenges and rewards of each, and providing insights on how leaders can effectively manage their teams to foster strong connections and drive organizational success.

The Importance of Employee Connection

Employee connection refers to the depth of engagement, trust, and sense of belonging that employees experience with their colleagues and within the broader organization. Far from being a peripheral aspect of workplace culture, employee connection is now widely recognized as a foundational pillar of both individual and organizational success. A strong sense of connection not only helps employees feel valued and understood, but it also cultivates a workplace environment where individuals are motivated to give their best effort.

When employees feel genuinely connected, they experience a greater sense of psychological safety—the confidence that they can express ideas, raise concerns, and take risks without fear of negative consequences. This safety fuels innovation, as team members are more likely to share creative solutions, experiment with new processes, and embrace change. Moreover, connection fosters open and honest communication. Employees are more apt to provide constructive feedback, seek help when needed, and work collaboratively to resolve conflicts. This leads to more effective teamwork and ensures that diverse perspectives are heard and respected.

The importance of employee connection also extends to overall employee well-being. Connected employees report higher levels of job satisfaction and emotional resilience. They are less likely to experience feelings of isolation, stress, or burnout, because they know they are supported by their peers and leaders. This sense of support encourages employees to remain engaged and committed to the organization's mission, even during challenging times.

In addition, organizations that prioritize employee connection consistently outperform those that do not. Studies show that teams with high levels of connection demonstrate increased productivity, stronger loyalty, and lower turnover rates. These benefits translate into significant cost savings, reduced absenteeism, and a reputation as an employer of choice, which attracts top talent. Ultimately, fostering employee connection is not just about making the workplace more pleasant—it is a vital driver of sustainable business performance, growth, and innovation.

Benefits of Strong Employee Connection

Increased Productivity

Employees who feel connected to their peers and leaders are more likely to be engaged in their work, leading to increased productivity and better performance. This engagement stems from a sense of belonging and purpose, which drives employees to go beyond in their roles.

Enhanced Collaboration

Strong connections facilitate open communication and collaboration, enabling teams to work more effectively toward common goals. When employees trust and respect each other, they are more willing to share knowledge, support one another, and work together to solve problems.

Improved Employee Retention

Organizations that prioritize employee connection often experience lower turnover rates. This is because connected employees feel valued and appreciated, reducing the likelihood of them seeking opportunities elsewhere. Lower turnover rates save costs associated with hiring and training

6

new employees and contribute to a more stable and experienced workforce.

Greater Innovation

A connected workforce is more likely to share ideas and take risks, fostering an environment of creativity and innovation. When employees feel safe and supported, they are more willing to experiment and propose innovative solutions, driving the organization forward.

Positive Workplace Culture

Leadership that promotes connection contributes to a positive organizational culture, making the workplace more enjoyable and fulfilling. A culture of connection is characterized by mutual respect, inclusiveness, and a shared commitment to the organization's values and goals.

Overview of All Eight Leadership Styles

In this chapter, we will identify the eight leadership styles— transformational, servant, authentic, autocratic, democratic, laissez-faire, transactional, and situational—highlighting their main traits and effects on employees and organizational success. Each style is briefly explained for comparison.

Understanding the challenges and benefits of these styles helps leaders build stronger teams and manage more effectively: Let's take a look:

1. ***Transformational Leadership:*** This style emphasizes inspiring and motivating employees to exceed their own self-interests for the sake of the organization. Transformational leaders build trust, create a shared vision, and encourage innovation and creative problem-solving.

2. ***Servant Leadership:*** Servant leaders prioritize the needs of their team members and focus on empowering and developing them. This style is built on empathy, humility, foresight, and stewardship, creating a culture of inclusion and resilience.

3. ***Authentic Leadership:*** Authentic leaders are genuine and transparent, fostering trust and connection through their authenticity. They lead with integrity, ethical decision-making, and self-awareness.

4. ***Autocratic Leadership:*** This top-down approach involves leaders making decisions unilaterally without much input from subordinates. It can be effective in situations requiring quick decision-making but may stifle creativity and employee engagement.

5. ***Democratic Leadership:*** Democratic leaders make decisions based on the input of each team member, promoting collaboration and shared responsibility. This style encourages participation and values diverse perspectives.

6. ***Laissez-Faire Leadership:*** A hands-off approach where leaders delegate most decision-making to team members. It can foster independence and innovation but may lead to a lack of direction if not managed properly.

7. ***Transactional Leadership***: This results-oriented leadership focuses on rewards and punishments based on performance. It is effective for achieving short-term goals but may not foster long-term engagement and development.

8. ***Situational Leadership:*** Situational leaders adapt their style based on the needs of the situation and the development level of the team. This flexible approach ensures that leadership is responsive to changing circumstances and individual needs.

Each of these styles has its own strengths and challenges, and effective leaders often blend elements from multiple styles to suit their specific organizational context and goals.

With today's rapidly evolving and interconnected world, leadership is no longer solely about authority or delegation; it is about creating environments where people feel seen, heard, and valued. As we reflect on the most effective leadership styles that promote connection, it becomes evident that leaders who emphasize empathy, collaboration, and authenticity are best positioned to foster meaningful relationships and inspire teams toward collective success.

At the heart of connective leadership is emotional intelligence. Leaders who excel in this realm understand that building trust is paramount. They are not only aware of their own emotions but also attuned to the feelings and motivations of others. This sensitivity allows them to engage with their teams on a deeper level, encouraging open communication and promoting a sense of psychological safety. When employees feel safe, they are more likely to contribute ideas, take risks, and innovate without fear of judgment or retribution.

Transformational leadership is another style that fosters deep connections. These leaders inspire by example, challenging their teams to reach higher levels of performance while providing the support needed to achieve those goals. By focusing on individual growth and aligning personal aspirations with organizational vision, transformational leaders create an environment where employees feel intrinsically motivated and engaged.

Servant leadership stands out as a model that inherently promotes connection. By prioritizing the needs of their team above their own, servant leaders demonstrate commitment to the well-being and development of their employees. This approach engenders loyalty and fosters a culture of mutual respect. Servant leaders listen more than they speak, guiding their teams with humility and compassion, which cultivates a sense of belonging and purpose.

Similarly, authenticity plays a crucial role in leadership that connects. Leaders who are genuine in their communication and actions inspire trust and transparency. Authentic leaders do not shy away from showing vulnerability, which in turn empowers their teams to be open and honest. This level of transparency fosters deeper connections because it humanizes the leader, creating a more relatable and cohesive working relationship.

Moreover, inclusive leadership is indispensable in a diverse and globalized workforce. Leaders who practice inclusively ensure that every voice is heard and that diverse perspectives are not only welcomed but actively sought. By valuing diversity of thought and experience, inclusive leaders break down silos, promote collaboration, and build stronger, more dynamic teams. This sense of inclusion strengthens team bonds and fosters an environment where connection thrives.

Different leadership styles can significantly influence the level of employee connection within an organization. Let's focus on a few effective styles that leaders can adopt.

Transformational Leadership

Leadership Mentee: Have you ever thought about why transformational leadership is so influential in organizations today?

Mike (Me): Absolutely. I believe it's because it goes beyond just hitting targets—it's about truly empowering and developing people. Transformational leaders focus on cultivating trust, inspiring teams, and encouraging growth at every level.

Leadership Mentee: Right, and they don't rely solely on their authority. They become role models, demonstrating the kind of integrity and commitment that inspires others.

Mike (Me): Exactly. They also motivate people by painting a compelling vision for the future—one that everyone can believe in and work toward. That kind of inspiration is contagious.

Leadership Mentee: And let's not forget intellectual stimulation. Transformational leaders are always encouraging innovation. They urge team members to challenge the status quo, think creatively, and come up with new solutions.

Mike (Me): Yes, and in addition to fostering innovation, they pay close attention to each person's growth. It's about seeing the individual, understanding their unique strengths, and helping them develop.

Leadership Mentee: Ultimately, this style of leadership connects people. It makes them feel valued, motivated, and engaged, which translates to greater productivity and satisfaction.

Mike (Me): That's why transformational leaders are so effective—they transform not just the organization, but the people within it.

Thoughts

- ***Building Trust:*** By demonstrating integrity and consistency, transformational leaders cultivate trust, essential for fostering strong connections.

- ***Creating a Shared Vision:*** Transformational leaders articulate a compelling vision that resonates with employees, aligning individual and organizational goals.

- ***Encouraging innovation and creative problem-solving:*** Involves fostering an environment where individuals are motivated to explore innovative ideas, think critically, and approach challenges from unconventional angles. It includes providing the freedom to experiment, take calculated risks, and learn from failures. This often requires a supportive culture that values curiosity, collaboration, and continuous learning, as well as offering resources, tools, and opportunities for individuals to develop and apply their creativity in solving complex problems.

Unlike transactional leadership, which focuses on rewards and punishments to achieve short-term goals, transformational leadership aims at fostering long-term change by aligning the values and goals of followers with those of the organization. By doing so, it creates a shared sense of purpose, which is often seen as a key driver of high-performing teams.

The Challenges and Rewards of Transformational Leadership

Challenges

1. ***High Expectations:*** Transformational leaders set lofty expectations for their teams, which can sometimes lead to stress and burnout. Employees may feel pressured to constantly perform at their best, which can be overwhelming without proper support and resources.

2. ***Emotional Investment:*** This leadership style requires a significant emotional investment from the leader. Transformational leaders must be deeply involved

with their team members, understanding their needs, motivations, and challenges. This can be emotionally draining and requires an elevated level of emotional intelligence.

3. ***Balancing Individual and Organizational Goals:*** Transformational leaders focus on both individual growth and organizational success. Balancing these two aspects can be challenging, as leaders must ensure that personal development aligns with the broader goals of the organization.

4. ***Sustaining Momentum:*** Maintaining the enthusiasm and motivation that transformational leadership generates can be difficult over the long term. Leaders must continuously inspire and engage their teams, which requires creativity and adaptability.

Rewards

Increased Innovation and Creativity: Transformational leadership fosters an environment of trust and psychological safety, where employees feel empowered to contribute ideas, take risks, and innovate. This leads to heightened creativity and problem-solving capabilities within teams, which are critical for maintaining competitiveness in today's fast-paced market.

1. ***Stronger Emotional Bonds***: Transformational leaders build strong emotional bonds with their teams, increasing employee engagement and satisfaction. Numerous studies have demonstrated a clear link between transformational leadership and lower employee turnover, higher job satisfaction, and greater organizational commitment.

2. ***Enhanced Organizational Performance***: In addition to employee well-being, transformational leadership positively impacts overall organizational performance metrics such as profitability, productivity, and innovation. Research across various industries has shown that organizations led by transformational

leaders tend to be more adaptable and resilient, which is especially important in times of crisis or uncertainty.

3. ***Personal and Organizational Growth***: When employees feel valued, supported, and inspired, they are more likely to go beyond in their roles. This drives both personal and organizational success, creating a virtuous cycle of growth and achievement.

Servant Leadership

As I reflect on my leadership journey, I realize I'm about 50% servant leader—and constantly working to grow that percentage. For me, servant leadership isn't just a management style; it's a philosophy and, honestly, a commitment to something bigger than myself.

I didn't always see it this way. At first, I thought leadership was about setting direction, motivating others, and driving toward results. But the more I've experienced, the more I've come to appreciate Robert K. Greenleaf's idea that true leadership starts with serving others. It's about focusing on the needs of my team, making sure they feel heard, supported, and empowered to grow—not just as employees, but as people.

Sometimes that's challenging. Balancing the drive for organizational success with caring for individuals isn't easy, and I'll admit, I sometimes revert to more traditional approaches. But each time I witness the positive impact of putting others first watching someone on my team step up, solve a problem creatively, or support a colleague, I'm reminded why I strive to lead this way.

I'm still on the journey, learning to listen more deeply and serve more selflessly. Maybe I'm not all the way there yet, but with every experience, that servant leader side of me grows stronger. And I genuinely believe that as I continue to nurture this philosophy, not only do I become a better leader, but my entire team thrives as well.

At its heart lies empathy, a profound ability to listen to and understand others' feelings, needs, and perspectives. A servant leader builds trust through transparency and authentic communication, ensuring that their team feels valued and heard. Humility is another cornerstone, where the leader recognizes that leadership is not about power or prestige, but about fostering the growth of others.

Equally important is foresight, a servant leader's ability to anticipate future consequences and lead with wisdom. Combined with stewardship, where leaders act as caretakers of their organization and its people, these principles ensure a holistic and forward-looking approach to leadership. Furthermore, servant leaders emphasize commitment to the growth of people, creating environments where others can thrive personally and professionally.

This distinct leadership philosophy requires a leader to take on the role of a healer in the workplace, mending relationships and building stronger teams. By putting the needs of their followers first, servant leaders foster a culture of inclusion, innovation, and resilience, where everyone is empowered to contribute to the greater good.

The implementation of servant leadership is not limited to theory or intention but can be seen across different industries, organizations, and societal structures. Through real-world examples and case studies, this book has demonstrated how servant leadership can lead to greater organizational success, employee satisfaction, and societal impact. Whether in business, education, healthcare, or non-profit sectors, servant leadership has consistently led to cultures of innovation, collaboration, and purpose-driven work.

For instance, companies like Southwest Airlines and Starbucks have integrated servant leadership principles into their corporate cultures, resulting in not only financial success but also in creating environments where employees feel valued, empowered, and motivated. Their leaders act not as distant figures of authority but as collaborators and mentors, inspiring their teams through service rather than control.

The Challenges and Rewards of Servant Leadership

Challenges

1. ***Personal Sacrifice***: Servant leadership requires an elevated level of personal sacrifice, patience, and dedication. Leaders must be willing to put the needs

of their team members above their own, which can be challenging for those accustomed to traditional models of power and control.

Humility and Selflessness: Adopting the humility and selflessness required of a servant leader can be difficult, especially in competitive and fast-paced industries. This approach may initially appear to slow down decision-making processes as it involves deeper listening, consensus-building, and personal engagement with team members.

2. ***Resistance to Change***: Leaders who are accustomed to traditional models of power and control may find it difficult to adopt the humility and selflessness required of a servant leader. This resistance can hinder the implementation of servant leadership principles.

3. ***Balancing Servant Leadership with Organizational Goals:*** Servant leaders must balance their focus on individual team members' needs with broader organizational goals. This can be challenging, as prioritizing personal development and well-being

may sometimes conflict with immediate business objectives.

Rewards

1. ***Higher Employee Retention***: Organizations that adopt servant leadership tend to have higher employee retention. Servant leaders build more resilient, agile, and motivated teams because they address the fundamental human need to feel valued and empowered.

2. ***Increased Innovation***: Servant leadership fosters a culture of inclusion, innovation, and resilience. By putting the needs of their followers first, servant leaders create an environment where everyone is empowered to contribute to the greater good.

3. ***Stronger Sense of Community***: Servant leaders build a stronger sense of community within their teams. This approach engenders loyalty and fosters a culture of mutual respect, leading to more resilient and motivated teams.

4. ***Broader Societal Impact***: The impact of servant leadership extends beyond the walls of the organization. When individuals are empowered through servant leadership, they carry those values into their communities and families, creating a ripple effect that can lead to broader societal change. In this sense, servant leadership is not just a business strategy, it is a movement toward a more compassionate, equitable, and sustainable world.

Authentic Leadership

I've been thinking about authentic leadership lately—what it really means to show up as yourself at work, even if you're not always firing at 100%. Honestly, I feel like I'm only operating at 30% most of the time, and that's okay. Authentic leadership isn't about being perfect or having endless energy; it's about being honest, transparent, and true to your values, even when you're running low.

When you lead authentically, you bring integrity and self-awareness to the table. It's about being real with your team, letting them see both your strengths and your struggles. For me, that means admitting when I'm feeling a bit off or stretched thin, but still doing my best to make decisions that align with what I believe in. That kind of openness builds trust—people know where you stand, and they feel safe to be themselves too.

So, even if I'm at 30%, as long as I'm showing up honestly, making thoughtful choices, and supporting my team, I'm still leading in a way that matters. I think that's the essence of authentic leadership: being present, being real, and doing what you can, no matter your energy level.

Integrity

Authentic leaders demonstrate high ethical standards and consistency in their actions. They make decisions based on their core values and principles, ensuring that their behavior aligns with their beliefs. This integrity fosters trust and respect among team members, who feel confident in their leader's reliability and honesty.

Transparency

These leaders are open and honest in their communication, sharing information and insights with their team members.

They are willing to admit mistakes and learn from them, creating a culture of openness and continuous improvement. Transparency helps build strong relationships and encourages collaboration within the team.

Self-Awareness

Authentic leaders have a deep understanding of their own strengths, weaknesses, and emotions. They are reflective and mindful, constantly seeking to improve themselves and their leadership skills. This self-awareness allows them to connect with their team members on a personal level and provide support tailored to individual needs.

Ethical Decision-Making

These leaders prioritize ethical considerations in their decision-making processes. They weigh the impact of their choices on their team, organization, and broader community, ensuring that their actions are responsible and just. Ethical decision-making reinforces the leader's integrity and strengthens the team's commitment to shared values.

Genuine Relationships

Authentic leaders build genuine relationships with their team members, based on mutual respect and trust. They take the time to understand everyone's unique perspectives and needs, fostering a sense of belonging and inclusion. By valuing and supporting their team members, authentic leaders create a positive and collaborative work environment.

The Challenges and Rewards of Authentic Leadership

Challenges

1. ***Vulnerability and Transparency:*** Authentic leaders must be open and honest, which can sometimes be perceived as a weakness. This level of transparency requires a high degree of self-awareness and the ability to admit mistakes, which can be challenging in a competitive environment.

2. ***Consistency:*** Maintaining consistent behavior that aligns with one's values and principles can be difficult, especially under pressure. Authentic leaders must

ensure their actions consistently reflect their core values, even when faced with tough decisions.

3. ***Building Trust:*** Establishing trust takes time and effort. Authentic leaders must demonstrate integrity and reliability consistently to build and maintain trust with their team members.

4. ***Balancing Authenticity and Professionalism:*** While being genuine is crucial, leaders must also balance their authenticity with professionalism. This means being true to oneself while also adhering to organizational norms and expectations.

Rewards

1. ***Increased Trust and Loyalty:*** Authentic leaders foster a culture of trust and loyalty. When employees see their leaders as genuine and trustworthy, they are more likely to be committed and loyal to the organization.

2. ***Enhanced Employee Engagement:*** Authentic leadership creates an environment where employees

feel valued and understood. This leads to higher levels of engagement, motivation, and job satisfaction.

3. ***Improved Team Performance:*** Teams led by authentic leaders often perform better. The trust and open communication fostered by authentic leadership lead to better collaboration, innovation, and overall team performance.

4. ***Positive Organizational Culture:*** Authentic leaders contribute to a positive organizational culture. Their integrity and ethical behavior set a standard for the entire organization, promoting a culture of honesty, respect, and inclusiveness.

Autocratic Leadership

Authentic leadership is a style that emphasizes genuineness and transparency, fostering trust and connection through the leader's authenticity. Authentic leaders lead with integrity, ethical decision-making, and self-awareness. They are genuine in their interactions and consistent in their actions, which helps build trust and credibility among their followers.

By being true to themselves and their values, authentic leaders create an environment where employees feel safe to express their own thoughts and ideas, leading to a more engaged and motivated team.

Detailed Style
of Authentic Leadership

Integrity

Authentic leaders demonstrate high ethical standards and consistency in their actions. They make decisions based on their core values and principles, ensuring that their behavior aligns with their beliefs. This integrity fosters trust and respect among team members, who feel confident in their leader's reliability and honesty.

Transparency

These leaders are open and honest in their communication, sharing information and insights with their team members. They are willing to admit mistakes and learn from them, creating a culture of openness and continuous improvement. Transparency helps build strong relationships and encourages collaboration within the team.

Self-Awareness

Authentic leaders have a deep understanding of their own strengths, weaknesses, and emotions. They are reflective and mindful, constantly seeking to improve themselves and their leadership skills. This self-awareness allows them to connect with their team members on a personal level and provide support tailored to individual needs.

Ethical Decision-Making

These leaders prioritize ethical considerations in their decision-making processes. They weigh the impact of their choices on their team, organization, and broader community, ensuring that their actions are responsible and just. Ethical decision-making reinforces the leader's integrity and strengthens the team's commitment to shared values.

Genuine Relationships

Authentic leaders build genuine relationships with their team members, based on mutual respect and trust. They take the time to understand everyone's unique perspectives and needs, fostering a sense of belonging and inclusion. By valuing and supporting their team members, authentic leaders create a positive and collaborative work environment.

On the back porch of a cabin, as we settled into our favorite chairs, the evening air thick with the scent of pines and shared history, my son, Jesse, asked me, "What do you think about Autocratic Leadership?". He had just finished leadership training with his company prior to our vacation!!

Me: You know, son, I've learned over the years that authentic leadership really comes down to being genuine and open with people. When a leader's honest and true to themselves, it lays the foundation for trust and good communication.

Jesse: I can see that, Dad. It seems like the leaders who have real integrity and self-awareness are the ones everyone trusts. People just know where they stand.

Me: That's right. And it's not just about honesty, either. Owning up to mistakes, letting your guard down now and then gives others permission to be themselves. That's when creativity really takes off.

Jesse: It definitely makes a difference. When folks feel safe and heard, they're more willing to share their ideas. That kind of environment breeds motivation and engagement.

Me: Exactly. The kind of leadership I've always respected is built on honesty, strong ethics, and authentic relationships. It's something I've tried to practice, though I know you have your own style that's just as meaningful.

Jesse: We do things a bit differently, but I think we agree on the basics. Authentic leadership creates a solid, positive, cooperative team.

Me: Well said, son.

The Challenges and Rewards of Autocratic Leadership

Challenges

1. ***Limited Employee Engagement:*** Autocratic leadership often involves making decisions unilaterally, with little input from team members. This can lead to low morale and a lack of engagement among employees, as they may feel their opinions and contributions are undervalued.

2. ***Stifled Creativity and Innovation:*** By encouraging input from team members, autocratic leaders may stifle creativity and innovation. Employees might be less likely to propose innovative ideas or solutions, fearing that their suggestions will be dismissed.

3. ***High Turnover Rates:*** The lack of employee involvement and recognition can lead to dissatisfaction and high turnover rates. Employees may seek opportunities elsewhere where they feel more valued and involved in decision-making processes.

4. ***Dependence on the Leader:*** Autocratic leadership can create a dependency on the leader for all decisions, which can be problematic if the leader is unavailable or leaves the organization. This dependency can hinder the development of leadership skills among team members.

5. ***Resistance to Change:*** Employees under autocratic leadership may resist change, as they are not involved in the decision-making process and may not

understand the reasons behind new initiatives. This can lead to a lack of buy-in and support for organizational changes.

Rewards

1. ***Quick Decision-Making:*** Autocratic leadership allows for quick decision-making, as the leader does not need to consult with team members. This can be beneficial in situations that require immediate action or during a crisis.

2. ***Clear Direction and Control:*** Autocratic leaders provide clear direction and maintain control over all aspects of the organization. This can lead to a well-organized and efficient operation, with everyone understanding their roles and responsibilities.

3. ***Consistency and Predictability:*** With a single leader making decisions, there is an elevated level of consistency and predictability in the organization's

operations. This can create a stable environment where employees know what to expect.

4. ***Effective in High-Stress Situations:*** In high-stress or emergency situations, autocratic leadership can be effective as it allows for decisive action without the need for lengthy discussions or consensus-building.

5. ***Strong Leadership Presence:*** Autocratic leaders often have a strong presence and can command respect and authority. This can be beneficial in maintaining discipline and order within the organization.

Overview of Democratic Leadership

Democratic leadership, also known as participative leadership, is a style that emphasizes collaboration and shared decision-making. In this approach, leaders involve team members in the decision-making process, valuing their input and fostering a sense of ownership and responsibility. Democratic leaders believe that collective wisdom leads to better decisions and more engaged employees. This style is particularly effective in environments where creativity, innovation, and diverse perspectives are valued.

Collaboration and Participation

Democratic leaders actively seek input from their team members, encouraging open discussions and brainstorming sessions. They create an environment where everyone feels comfortable sharing their ideas and opinions. This collaborative approach not only leads to more innovative solutions but also fosters a sense of belonging and commitment among employees.

Empowerment and Trust

By involving team members in decision-making, democratic leaders empower them to take ownership of their work. This trust in employees' abilities boosts their confidence and motivation, leading to higher levels of engagement and productivity. Empowerment also encourages employees to develop their skills and take on new challenges.

Transparency and Communication

Democratic leaders prioritize transparent communication, ensuring that team members are informed about the organization's goals, challenges, and decisions. They provide regular updates and encourage feedback, creating a culture of openness and trust. This transparency helps build strong relationships and fosters a sense of accountability.

Inclusivity and Diversity

Democratic leadership values diverse perspectives and experiences. Leaders actively seek out and include voices from diverse backgrounds, ensuring that decisions are well-rounded and considerate of various viewpoints. This inclusivity not only enhances the quality of decisions but also promotes a culture of respect and equality.

Shared Responsibility

In a democratic leadership style, responsibility is shared among team members. Leaders delegate tasks and encourage collaboration, ensuring that everyone contributes to the success of the team. This shared responsibility fosters a sense of unity and collective achievement.

Looking back over my career, I've had more than a few bosses who embodied the democratic leadership style. I remember sitting in meeting after meeting with them—

sometimes it felt like we'd never reach a decision! We'd discuss every angle, gather input from the whole team, and while I appreciated the openness, I sometimes found myself wishing for a bit more decisiveness. There were moments when it seemed like consensus was more important than progress. Still, those experiences taught me a lot about collaboration and the value of every voice at the table, even if the process could be exhausting at times.

Challenges and Rewards of Democratic Leadership

Challenges

1. ***Time-Consuming Decision-Making:*** Democratic leadership involves seeking input from team members, which can slow down the decision-making process. While this approach ensures that diverse perspectives are considered, it can be inefficient in situations that require quick decisions.

2. ***Potential for Conflict:*** Encouraging open discussions and diverse viewpoints can sometimes lead to

disagreements and conflicts within the team. Managing these conflicts requires strong mediation skills and the ability to foster a collaborative environment.

3. ***Balancing Participation and Authority:*** Democratic leaders must strike a balance between involving team members in decision-making and maintaining their authority. Over-reliance on consensus can lead to indecisiveness, while too much control can undermine the participative nature of this leadership style.

4. ***Risk of Groupthink:*** While democratic leadership values diverse perspectives, there is a risk of groupthink if team members prioritize harmony over critical thinking. Leaders must be vigilant in encouraging independent thought and challenging assumptions.

Rewards

1. ***Enhanced Employee Engagement:*** By involving team members in decision-making, democratic leaders foster a sense of ownership and responsibility. This empowerment leads to higher levels of engagement, motivation, and job satisfaction.

2. ***Increased Innovation and Creativity:*** Democratic leadership encourages open discussions and brainstorming sessions, which can lead to innovative solutions and creative problem-solving. Diverse perspectives contribute to more well-rounded decisions.

3. ***Stronger Team Cohesion:*** Collaboration and participation in decision-making processes build trust and strengthen relationships within the team. This sense of unity and collective achievement enhances team cohesion and morale.

4. ***Improved Decision Quality:*** By considering input from various team members, democratic leaders can make more informed and well-rounded decisions.

This approach leverages the collective wisdom of the team, leading to better outcomes.

Overview of Laissez-Faire Leadership

Laissez-faire leadership, also known as delegative leadership, is a hands-off approach where leaders provide minimal direct supervision and allow team members to make decisions and solve problems independently. This style is characterized by a high degree of autonomy and trust in employees' abilities to manage their own work. Laissez-faire leaders believe that the best results come from giving employees the freedom to innovate and take ownership of their tasks. **Allow me to introduce the man who shaped so much of who I am—my dad. I spent my summers and after-school hours working for him, and this is truly his style!**

In a laissez-faire leadership environment, leaders provide the necessary resources and support but refrain from micromanaging or intervening in day-to-day activities. This approach can be highly effective in teams with experienced, initiative-taking, and skilled individuals who thrive on independence. It fosters a culture of creativity and innovation, as employees are encouraged to explore innovative ideas and solutions without constant oversight.

However, laissez-faire leadership also comes with its challenges. Without clear guidance and direction, some team members may struggle with a lack of structure and accountability. This can lead to inconsistencies in performance and a potential decline in productivity. Therefore, it is essential for laissez-faire leaders to strike a balance between providing autonomy and ensuring that team members have the support and resources they need to succeed.

Overall, laissez-faire leadership can be a powerful tool for fostering innovation and empowering employees, but it requires a careful balance to ensure that the team remains focused and productive.

Challenges and Rewards
of Laissez-Faire Leadership

Challenges

1. ***Lack of Direction and Accountability:*** One of the primary challenges of laissez-faire leadership is the potential for a lack of direction and accountability. Without clear guidance and oversight, team members may struggle to stay focused and meet deadlines. This can lead to inconsistencies in performance and a decline in productivity.

2. ***Risk of Underperformance:*** In a laissez-faire environment, employees who require more structure and support may underperform. This leadership style assumes that all team members are initiative-taking and capable of managing their own tasks, which may not always be the case.

3. ***Communication Gaps:*** With minimal direct supervision, communication gaps can arise. Vital information may not be effectively shared, leading to misunderstandings and a lack of cohesion within the team.

4. ***Difficulty in Managing Diverse Teams:*** Laissez-faire leadership can be challenging when managing diverse teams with varying levels of experience and expertise. Some team members may thrive in an autonomous environment, while others may feel overwhelmed and unsupported.

Rewards

1. ***Fostering Innovation and Creativity:*** Laissez-faire leadership can foster a culture of innovation and creativity. By giving employees the freedom to explore innovative ideas and solutions, this leadership style encourages experimentation and out-of-the-box thinking.

2. ***Empowerment and Ownership:*** This leadership style empowers employees by giving them autonomy and trust to manage their own work. This sense of ownership can boost motivation and job satisfaction, as employees feel more responsible for their contributions.

3. ***Development of Leadership Skills:*** In a laissez-faire environment, employees can develop their leadership skills. By taking on more responsibility and making decisions independently, team members can grow and enhance their capabilities.

4. ***High Job Satisfaction:*** Employees who thrive on independence and self-direction often experience high job satisfaction in a laissez-faire environment. The freedom to manage their own tasks and make decisions can lead to a more fulfilling work experience.

Overview of Transactional Leadership

Transactional leadership is a style that focuses on structure, rewards, and performance. Leaders who adopt this approach set clear goals and expectations for their team members and provide rewards or punishments based on their performance. This purposeful leadership style is effective for achieving short-term goals and maintaining order within an organization. Transactional leaders emphasize the importance of following established procedures and meeting specific targets.

Clear Expectations and Goals

Transactional leaders set specific, measurable, achievable, relevant, and time-bound (SMART) goals for their team members. They clearly define roles and responsibilities, ensuring that everyone understands what is expected of them. This clarity helps employees stay focused and motivated to achieve their objectives.

Rewards and Punishments

This leadership style relies heavily on a system of rewards and punishments to motivate employees. Leaders provide incentives such as bonuses, promotions, or recognition for meeting or exceeding goals. Conversely, they may impose penalties or disciplinary actions for failing to meet expectations. This approach ensures that employees are held accountable for their performance.

Structured Environment

Transactional leaders create a structured environment where procedures and protocols are strictly followed. They prioritize efficiency and consistency, ensuring that tasks are completed according to established guidelines. This structure helps maintain order and predictability within the organization.

Performance Monitoring

Transactional leaders closely monitor the performance of their team members. They use metrics and key performance indicators (KPIs) to track progress and identify areas for improvement. Regular performance reviews and feedback sessions help employees stay on track and continuously improve their performance.

Short-Term Focus

This leadership style is particularly effective for achieving short-term goals and managing routine tasks. Transactional leaders focus on immediate results and operational efficiency, making it suitable for environments where consistency and reliability are crucial.

Challenges and Rewards
of Transactional Leadership

Challenges

1. ***Limited Creativity and Innovation:*** Transactional leadership may stifle creativity and innovation, as it emphasizes following established procedures and meeting specific targets. Employees may feel restricted and less inclined to propose innovative ideas or solutions.

2. ***Dependence on Rewards:*** This leadership style relies heavily on external rewards to motivate employees. Over time, employees may become dependent on these incentives and lose intrinsic motivation, leading to decreased engagement and satisfaction.

3. ***Short-Term Focus:*** Transactional leadership is effective for achieving short-term goals but may not foster long-term engagement and development. Leaders may struggle to inspire employees to think beyond immediate tasks and contribute to the organization's long-term vision.

Rewards

1. ***Clear Direction and Accountability:*** Transactional leadership provides clear direction and accountability, ensuring that employees understand their roles and responsibilities. This clarity helps maintain order and predictability within the organization.

2. ***Efficient Performance Management:*** By closely monitoring performance and providing regular feedback, transactional leaders can quickly identify and address issues. This approach helps maintain elevated levels of productivity and operational efficiency.

3. ***Achievement of Short-Term Goals:*** Transactional leadership is particularly effective for achieving short-term goals and managing routine tasks. Leaders can ensure that targets are met, and procedures are followed, leading to consistent and reliable results.

Overview of Situational Leadership

Situational leadership is a flexible and adaptive leadership style that emphasizes the need for leaders to adjust their approach based on the specific circumstances and the development level of their team members. This leadership style, developed by Paul Hersey and Ken Blanchard, recognizes that there is no one-size-fits-all approach to leadership. Instead, effective leaders must assess the situation and the needs of their team to determine the most appropriate leadership style to employ. **In my view, half of all leaders possess the necessary abilities, while the other half are simply not capable of fulfilling the role at all.**

Assessment of Team Members

Situational leaders begin by assessing the competence and commitment of their team members. This involves understanding their skills, experience, and motivation levels. Based on this assessment, leaders can determine the appropriate level of direction and support needed.

Adapting Leadership Style

Situational leaders adapt their leadership style to match the development level of their team members. Hersey and Blanchard identified four primary leadership styles within the situational leadership model:

Directing

High directive and low supportive behavior. This style is used when team members are inexperienced or lack confidence. The leader provides clear instructions and closely supervises tasks.

Coaching

High directive and high supportive behavior. This style is used when team members have some competence but still need guidance and encouragement. The leader provides direction while also supporting and motivating the team.

Supporting

Low directive and high supportive behavior. This style is used when team members are competent but may lack confidence or motivation. The leader provides support and encouragement, allowing team members to take more responsibility for their tasks.

Delegating

Low directive and low supportive behavior. This style is used when team members are highly competent and motivated. The leader delegates tasks and responsibilities, allowing team members to work independently.

Flexibility and Responsiveness

Situational leaders must be flexible and responsive to changing circumstances. They continuously assess the situation and adjust their leadership style as needed. This adaptability ensures that the team always receives the appropriate level of guidance and support.

Communication and Feedback: Effective communication is crucial in situational leadership. Leaders must clearly communicate expectations, provide feedback, and listen to their team members' concerns. Regular feedback helps team members understand their progress and areas for improvement.

Challenges and Rewards
of Situational Leadership

Challenges

1. ***Complexity and Time-Consuming:*** Assessing the development level of each team member and adapting the leadership style accordingly can be complex and time-consuming. Leaders must invest

significant effort in understanding their team members and the specific needs of each situation.

2. ***Consistency:*** Maintaining consistency in leadership while adapting to different situations can be challenging. Leaders must ensure that their approach remains fair and balanced, even as they adjust their style to meet the needs of their team.

3. ***Skill and Experience:*** Situational leadership requires an elevated level of skill and experience. Leaders must be adept at assessing situations, making quick decisions, and effectively communicating with their team members.

Rewards

1. ***Enhanced Team Performance:*** By adapting their leadership style to meet the specific needs of their team members, situational leaders can enhance overall team performance. This tailored approach ensures that team members receive the appropriate

level of guidance and support, leading to higher productivity and job satisfaction.

2. ***Employee Development:*** Situational leadership promotes the development of team members by providing the right level of support and challenge. This approach helps employees build their skills, confidence, and motivation, leading to personal and professional growth.

3. ***Flexibility and Adaptability:*** Situational leadership fosters a flexible and adaptable work environment. Leaders and team members learn to respond effectively to changing circumstances, which enhances the team's ability to navigate challenges and seize opportunities.

Summary of Leadership Styles

In this chapter, we explored eight distinct leadership styles, each with its unique characteristics and impact on employee connection and organizational success. Understanding these styles is crucial for leaders who aim to foster strong connections and engagement within their teams.

Conclusion

When I embarked on my journey in leadership, there were no formal frameworks or labels to guide me—just intuition and the lessons I carried from observing others. Early on, I found myself drawing wisdom from the poor leadership examples I encountered, using them as a guide for what not to do. Combined with the invaluable teachings passed down by my father and grandfather, these experiences became the compass that directed my path, often relying on instinct to navigate the challenges and uncertainties of leadership.

My grandfather, Louis Bryant, was more than just a trash collector for the City of Detroit—he was the backbone of our family and community. For two decades, he rose before dawn, lacing up his work boots and braving every kind of weather, determined to provide for us through sheer perseverance and dignity. When he retired, he poured his energy into purchasing and carefully renovating old, neglected homes, breathing new life into them and creating safe, welcoming spaces for new families. He also became the steadfast caretaker and deacon of our church, a place rich with a century of our family's memories.

Looking back, I realize how much I could have gained from understanding the leadership styles mentioned in this section sooner. It would have spared me countless missteps and provided clarity during moments of doubt. Each leadership style holds unique strengths and challenges, and truly effective leaders embrace a blend of approaches, adapting them not just to achieve organizational goals but to inspire trust, connection, and genuine growth among their teams.

As I reflect on this, I hope these insights give you more than just a framework—they offer a deeper understanding of how leadership shapes not just teams, but lives. Do you find yourself resonating with these ideas and seeing how they might transform the way employees engage, grow, and feel valued within your organization?

2

Things You Must Understand

Full Transparency - for years, I embraced a leadership style that focused solely on efficiency and results, believing that my role was simply to provide direction and ensure tasks were completed. It was a pragmatic approach, but one that left so much untapped potential within my team. I failed to see the transformative power of sharing the *"why"*, the essence and purpose behind every action. Productivity alone seemed like the ultimate benchmark of success, yet it did not foster the genuine connection and enthusiasm I longed to see in my team.

It was only after reflecting deeply on my leadership journey that I began to recognize the profound impact of transparency and shared vision. When leaders invest the time to articulate the reasons behind their decisions, they inspire more than compliance—they ignite passion, creativity, and commitment. Offering context transforms tasks from mere obligations into opportunities for growth and innovation. It creates a vibrant atmosphere where individuals not only understand their roles but feel genuinely connected to the larger purpose of the organization. These moments of clarity can spark enthusiasm and transform a group of individuals into a united, purpose-driven team.

Communication: The Cornerstone of Connection

Effective communication is the foundation upon which strong employee connections are built. It is the glue that holds teams together, fostering trust, collaboration, and a sense of belonging. When leaders prioritize clear, open, and honest communication, they create an environment where employees feel valued, understood, and motivated to contribute their best work. Here's a detailed summary of why communication is the cornerstone of employee connection:

Building Trust and Credibility

Transparent communication is fundamental for establishing trust and credibility within a team. When leaders communicate openly and honestly, they demonstrate integrity and dependability. This approach reassures employees that they are kept informed about important changes, organizational goals, and challenges. Regular updates and opportunities for open dialogue further strengthen this trust, cultivating a culture of openness and mutual respect.

Enhancing Collaboration and Teamwork

Clear communication is key to effective collaboration and teamwork. When team members have a solid understanding of their roles, responsibilities, and shared objectives, they can coordinate their efforts more efficiently. Open communication channels allow ideas and information to circulate freely, enabling teams to solve problems creatively and work together seamlessly. This cooperative environment not only boosts productivity but also deepens the connections between team members.

Promoting Employee Engagement and Motivation

Employees who feel heard and appreciated are naturally more engaged and motivated. Attentive listening—where leaders genuinely focus on what employees say and respond thoughtfully—demonstrates that everyone's input is valued. This active engagement creates a sense of belonging and commitment to the organization. Offering constructive feedback, whether positive or developmental, guides employees in their growth and reinforces their motivation and confidence.

Reducing Misunderstandings and Conflicts

Consistent and direct communication minimizes confusion and potential conflicts within a team. Clearly expressing expectations, goals, and responsibilities leaves little room for misinterpretation. This clarity helps to prevent disagreements that can stem from misunderstandings and ensures everyone is aligned with organizational objectives. When conflicts do occur, an open line of communication allows for timely resolution, maintaining a harmonious and productive work environment.

Fostering a Positive Workplace Culture

A workplace built on open and honest communication nurtures a positive environment where employees feel comfortable sharing their ideas and perspectives. This culture of inclusiveness and respect encourages innovation and collaboration. Leaders who model transparent communication inspire these same values throughout the organization, reinforcing a foundation of trust and mutual regard.

Supporting Change and Adaptability

In a rapidly changing business world, strong communication is essential for guiding teams through transitions. Leaders who clearly explain upcoming changes, the reasoning behind them, and the expected outcomes help employees adjust and embrace new directions. This transparency reduces resistance and encourages adaptability, empowering employees to confidently face challenges and drive organizational success.

Communication and Transparency

Additionally, effective communication and transparency contribute to a vibrant workplace culture. When employees know their voices are heard and their efforts are recognized, they are more engaged and motivated. This engagement results in higher productivity and performance, with employees more invested in both their own success and that of the organization.

While building a culture of communication and transparency can be challenging, the rewards are significant. Organizations that champion these values foster motivated, engaged teams that drive long-term success and innovation.

This principle has been foundational in my own leadership journey—whether working with hourly staff, managers, mentees, or mentors. Prioritizing honest communication has helped me build deeper connections and cultivate mutual growth, inspiring all of us to become the best versions of ourselves.

In summary, communication is the cornerstone of employee connection. It builds trust and credibility, enhances collaboration and teamwork, promotes engagement and motivation, reduces misunderstandings and conflicts, fosters a positive workplace culture, and supports change and adaptability. By prioritizing clear, open, and honest communication, leaders can create a connected and engaged workforce that drives organizational success.

3

Fostering a Diverse Workplace

Inclusivity and diversity are essential components of a thriving workplace. They contribute to a positive organizational culture, enhance creativity and innovation, and improve employee satisfaction and retention. Leaders play a crucial role in fostering an inclusive and diverse environment by promoting diverse perspectives, addressing bias, and celebrating differences. Here's a detailed overview of how leaders can achieve this, along with examples to illustrate these practices.

Promoting Diverse Perspectives

Leaders should actively encourage diverse perspectives within the workplace, understanding that varied experiences and viewpoints enrich discussions and decision-making. This can be achieved by:

1. ***Creating Diverse Teams:*** Forming teams with individuals from diverse backgrounds and experiences foster collaboration and innovation. For example, a tech company might assemble a project team that includes members from diverse cultural backgrounds, genders, and age groups to develop a new product. This diversity can lead to more creative solutions and a product that appeals to a broader audience.

2. ***Valuing Contributions:*** Recognizing and celebrating the unique contributions of each employee reinforces their sense of belonging. For instance, a manager might highlight the achievements of team members during meetings, ensuring that everyone's efforts are acknowledged and appreciated.

3. ***Addressing Bias:*** Leaders must actively work to identify and address bias within the organization. This involves:

   - ***Providing Training***: Implementing training programs on unconscious bias to raise awareness and promote equitable practices. For example, a company might conduct workshops where employees learn about the impact of unconscious bias and strategies to mitigate it.

- ***Encouraging Open Dialogue:*** Creating safe spaces for discussions about diversity, equity, and inclusion fosters a culture of understanding. An example could be hosting regular forums where employees can share their experiences and discuss ways to improve inclusivity within the organization.

Celebrating Differences

Leaders should celebrate differences within the workforce, promoting connection by:

- ***Recognizing Cultural Events:*** Acknowledging and celebrating cultural holidays and events fosters appreciation for diversity. For instance, an organization might celebrate Diwali, Lunar New Year, or Black History Month with events and activities that educate employees about these cultures.

- ***Encouraging Employee Resource Groups:*** Supporting the formation of employee resource groups (ERGs) that focus on shared experiences provides a sense of community and connection. For example, a company might have ERGs for women, LGBTQ+ employees, veterans, and other groups, offering a platform for support and advocacy.

Examples

Creating Diverse Teams

A multinational corporation forms a product development team with members from various countries, ensuring that diverse cultural perspectives are considered in the design process. This diversity leads to a product that is well-received in multiple markets, demonstrating the value of diverse viewpoints.

Providing Training

A financial services firm implements a comprehensive training program on unconscious bias. Employees participate in interactive workshops where they learn to recognize their biases and develop strategies to counteract them. As a result, the company sees an improvement in hiring practices and a more inclusive workplace culture.

Recognizing Cultural Events

A healthcare organization celebrates Hispanic Heritage Month by organizing events that highlight the contributions of Hispanic employees and educate the workforce about Hispanic culture. These events include guest speakers, cultural performances, and food tastings, fostering a greater appreciation for diversity.

Encouraging Employee Resource Groups

A tech company supports the formation of an LGBTQ+ employee resource group. The group organizes events, provides mentorship, and advocates for policies that support LGBTQ+ employees. This initiative helps create a more inclusive environment and attracts top talent from the LGBTQ+ community.

4

Emotional Intelligence and Empathy

Emotional Intelligence (EI) and empathy are closely related but distinct concepts that play a significant role in personal and professional interactions.

Emotional Intelligence involves the ability to recognize, understand, manage, and influence one's own emotions and the emotions of others. It consists of several key components:

1. *Self-awareness:* Recognizing and understanding one's own emotions.
2. *Self-regulation:* Managing emotions in a healthy way.
3. *Motivation:* Using emotions to drive oneself towards goals.
4. *Social skills:* Understanding and sharing the feelings of others.
5. *Empathy:* Managing relationships and building networks effectively.

Research shows that individuals with high EI and empathy tend to have better interpersonal relationships, leadership skills, and conflict resolution abilities. They are also better equipped to manage stress and adapt to change.

Self-Awareness

Self-awareness is the foundation of emotional intelligence. It involves recognizing and understanding one's own emotions, strengths, weaknesses, values, and motivations. Self-aware leaders are conscious of how their emotions affect their behavior and decision-making. This awareness allows them to connect more effectively with employees by modeling emotional regulation and recognizing their impact on others. By demonstrating calmness and composure during challenging situations, they inspire employees to manage their emotions. Additionally, understanding how their emotions and actions influence team dynamics helps foster a supportive environment.

Self-Regulation

Self-regulation is the ability to manage and control one's emotions in a healthy and constructive manner. Leaders who can regulate their emotions are less likely to react impulsively and more likely to respond thoughtfully to challenging situations. This ability to stay composed under pressure sets a positive example for employees and helps maintain a stable and productive work environment. Self-regulation also involves being adaptable and open to change, which is essential for navigating the complexities of the modern workplace.

Motivation

Motivation in the context of emotional intelligence refers to the inner drive to achieve goals and pursue excellence. Leaders with high emotional intelligence are intrinsically motivated and enthusiastic about their work. They set lofty standards for themselves and their teams, inspiring others to strive for excellence. This motivation is not driven by external rewards but by a genuine desire to make a positive impact. Motivated leaders are resilient in the face of setbacks and challenges, and their enthusiasm is contagious, fostering a culture of dedication and perseverance within the team.

Social Skills

Social skills are the ability to manage relationships, build networks, and navigate social complexities. Leaders with strong social skills are effective communicators, negotiators, and conflict resolvers. They excel at building and maintaining positive relationships with employees, peers, and stakeholders. Socially skilled leaders are adept at fostering teamwork and collaboration, creating an inclusive and cohesive work environment. They are also skilled at managing conflicts constructively, ensuring that disagreements are resolved in a way that strengthens relationships rather than damaging them.

Empathy

Empathy is the ability to understand and share the feelings of others. Leaders who practice empathy foster stronger connections by recognizing employee needs and building trust. Being attuned to employees' feelings and needs allows leaders to respond appropriately and supportively. Demonstrating empathy helps create an environment of trust, encouraging open communication and collaboration. Empathetic leaders are skilled at reading non-verbal cues and understanding the underlying emotions behind their team members' words and actions. This deep understanding enables them to provide personalized support and address concerns effectively.

Understanding Empathy Across Disciplines

Empathy, a multifaceted and dynamic skill, is pivotal in various fields, from psychology and neuroscience to social science, healthcare, and business. Its significance lies in its ability to enhance communication, build relationships, and foster prosocial behavior.

Psychological Perspectives

In psychology, empathy is often viewed as a skill that can be developed and refined. It is crucial for effective communication and relationship-building. Researchers have identified specific brain areas, such as the mirror neuron system, which are activated when people experience empathy. This neural basis underscores the inherent capacity for empathy within the human brain, suggesting that with practice and intention, individuals can enhance their empathetic abilities.

Social Science Insights

From a social science perspective, empathy plays a vital role in reducing conflicts, enhancing cooperation, and promoting prosocial behavior. It is a key factor in leadership and workplace dynamics, where empathetic leaders tend to have more engaged and satisfied teams. By understanding and addressing the emotions and perspectives of others, leaders can create a more harmonious and productive work environment.

Emotional Intelligence and Connection

Emotional intelligence (EI) is a critical skill for effective leadership and fostering strong employee connections.

It involves the ability to recognize, understand, manage, and influence one's own emotions and the emotions of others. Leaders with high emotional intelligence are better equipped to navigate the complexities of interpersonal relationships, create a positive work environment, and drive organizational success. Here's a detailed understanding of the key components of emotional intelligence and their impact on leadership:

Healthcare Applications

In healthcare, empathy is essential for building trust and improving patient outcomes. Empathetic communication helps patients feel heard and understood, leading to better adherence to treatment plans and overall satisfaction. Studies have shown that healthcare providers who display empathy tend to have fewer malpractice claims and better relationships with patients. This highlights the critical role of empathy in patient care and the overall effectiveness of healthcare delivery.

Business Relevance

In business settings, empathy is a key component of emotional intelligence, which is critical for effective leadership. Leaders who demonstrate empathy can foster a positive workplace culture, improve employee engagement, and navigate conflicts more successfully. Empathy is also linked to increased creativity and collaboration, as employees feel more valued and understood. This connection between empathy and business success underscores the importance of cultivating empathetic leadership in the corporate world.

Developing Empathy

Research across these fields emphasizes that empathy can be developed through training and practice. For healthcare professionals, this might include workshops on active listening and patient-centered communication. In business, empathy training can involve role-playing exercises and feedback to improve people skills. By investing in empathy development, individuals and organizations can enhance their ability to connect with others, leading to more effective and fulfilling interactions.

Emotional intelligence is the key to both personal and professional success.

Stephen R. Covey

——————))•((——————

5

Building Trust and Respect

When starting a new role, I prioritize establishing clarity and alignment from the outset. Within the first week, I initiate meetings to discuss the directives and mission laid out by senior leadership. These conversations are instrumental in breaking down overarching objectives into actionable strategies tailored to our team's unique strengths and challenges. I actively encourage feedback during these discussions, creating an atmosphere where everyone's perspective is valued. This collaborative approach not only fosters trust but also ensures that we are united in our vision and approach. As the team aligns itself with these goals, efficiency and engagement become natural outcomes, setting the stage for long-term success.

Trust is the cornerstone of any meaningful relationship, especially between employees and their leaders. When employees have confidence in their leaders, they become more engaged, willing to take calculated risks, and receptive to feedback. Trust is cultivated through consistent, dependable, and ethical behavior. Leaders can nurture trust by:

- Demonstrating consistency in their actions and decisions.
- Fulfilling promises and commitments.
- Acknowledging mistakes and learning from them.

Trust is indeed a fundamental component of connection in any relationship, whether personal or professional. It creates a safe space where individuals feel valued and respected, enabling open communication and collaboration. Here are a few key points on how trust acts as the foundation of connection:

Trust fosters a sense of security, allowing individuals to express themselves openly without fear of judgment. It encourages collaboration, as people are more likely to work together when they trust one another. Additionally, it enhances communication, as individuals feel more comfortable sharing their thoughts and ideas.

Creating a culture of mutual respect involves recognizing the unique contributions of each employee and treating everyone with dignity. Leaders who model respectful behavior and promote inclusiveness are more likely to have teams that feel connected and motivated.

Building trust and respect involves several key principles:

1. ___Communication:___ Open, honest, and clear communication fosters understanding and reduces misunderstandings. Actively listening to others is also crucial.

2. ___Consistency:___ Being dependable and consistent in actions and words helps establish credibility. Following through on commitments reinforce trust.

3. **Integrity:** Demonstrating honesty and ethical behavior is fundamental. People are more likely to trust those who act with integrity.

4. ___Empathy:___ Understanding and valuing others' perspectives builds respect. Showing empathy helps create strong connections.

5. *__Accountability:__* Taking responsibility for one's, actions and decisions reinforces trust. Acknowledging mistakes and learning from them promotes growth.

6. *__Support:__* Being supportive and showing appreciation for others' contributions fosters a positive environment, enhancing mutual respect.

7. *__Boundaries:__* Respecting personal boundaries and differences cultivates a culture of respect, allowing individuals to feel safe and valued.

In essence, trust serves as the very foundation upon which meaningful connections are built. It paves the way for stronger relationships, fosters collaboration, and nurtures a profound sense of community. Without trust, even the most well-intentioned efforts can falter, as it is the invisible thread that binds individuals together in understanding and harmony. Cultivating trust and respect is not an overnight task—it requires patience, consistency, and a genuine commitment to valuing others.

Whether in personal relationships or professional settings, the act of building trust demands an openness to vulnerability and a willingness to grow alongside others. Respect, on the other hand, blossoms when people feel seen, heard, and appreciated for their unique selves. Together, trust and respect create an environment where people can thrive, feel secure, and truly connect on a deeper level. Though the journey to fostering these qualities may be challenging, the rewards stronger, more compassionate, and united community are undoubtedly worth the effort.

Creating a Culture of Mutual Respect

A culture of mutual respect is crucial in any organization or community and involves several key strategies:

1. *Lead by Example:* Leaders should model respectful behavior in all interactions, demonstrating the importance of respect in the workplace.

2. *Clear Communication:* Encourage open and honest communication. This includes active listening and providing constructive feedback without criticism.

3. *Training and Development:* Implement training programs that focus on diversity, inclusion, and

conflict resolution. This can help staff understand and appreciate different perspectives.

4. ***Recognize Contributions:*** Acknowledge and celebrate the achievements of individuals and teams. Recognition fosters a sense of belonging and appreciation.

5. ***Encourage Collaboration:*** Create opportunities for teamwork and collaboration across different departments. This can enhance relationships and understanding among staff.

6. ***Set Expectations:*** Clearly define and communicate behavioral expectations. Policies on respect should be in place and enforced consistently.

7. ***Feedback Mechanisms:*** Establish channels for employees to provide feedback on their experiences and any issues related to respect. Ensure that this feedback is taken seriously and addressed.

8. ***Conflict Resolution:*** Provide resources and support for resolving conflicts in a respectful and constructive

manner. This may include mediation or counseling services.

9. ***Celebrating Diversity:*** Foster is an inclusive environment that respects and values diversity in all forms, including race, gender, age, and experiences.

10. ***Regular Assessment:*** Periodically assess the workplace culture through surveys or focus groups to identify areas for improvement in mutual respect.

In summary, by cultivating a culture of mutual respect. These strategies can cultivate an environment where mutual respect thrives, leading to enhanced morale, collaboration, and overall productivity.

Example Exercise
Building Trust and Respect

When I join a new team, one of the most meaningful things I focus on is building trust and respect. Trust, to me, is the foundation of every strong relationship, it's what allows us to connect on a deeper level, work together seamlessly, and feel like we're part of something bigger. I believe trust is earned through actions that show consistency, integrity, and care. Respect, on the other hand, is about truly seeing the value in every person, appreciating their unique strengths, and treating them with dignity. When trust and respect come together, they create an environment where people feel empowered, safe, and genuinely valued. This, in turn, makes communication and collaboration not just possible, but meaningful.

Objective
To explore strategies for building trust and respect within a team.

Steps

1. Define trust and respect in the context of personal, professional, and organizational relationships.
2. Discuss the importance of trust and respect for effective communication, teamwork, and leadership.

Building Trust and Respect in Different Contexts

- Discuss how leaders can model trustworthy behavior and show respect.

- Explore the impact of different leadership styles (e.g., transformational vs. transactional) on trust and respect.

- In groups, develop strategies for promoting open communication and collaboration.

- Discuss the role of conflict resolution in maintaining trust and respect.

Challenges and Barriers

1. *Identify common barriers* to trust and respect, such as communication breakdowns, cultural differences, and personal biases.

2. *Develop strategies to address and overcome these challenges*, such as active listening, bias training, and transparent decision-making processes.

Strategies and Best Practices

1. *For individuals:* Focus on personal accountability, emotional intelligence, and consistent behavior.

2. *For teams:* Establish clear norms, promote shared goals, and recognize contributions.

Reflection

1. Summarize the key points discussed.

2. Reflect on the importance of trust and respect and the strategies developed.

3. Discuss the next steps for implementing these strategies within the team.

Conclusion

"Today's activity was a valuable opportunity for us to connect and strengthen the foundation of trust and respect within our team. By actively listening, sharing our thoughts, and working collaboratively, we have demonstrated our commitment to open communication and mutual understanding. Trust and respect are essential elements for any successful team, and our willingness to engage in this process highlights the positive dynamic we are building together. Moving forward, let us continue to apply these principles in our daily interactions, supporting each other and fostering a culture where everyone feels valued and heard. Together, we can achieve remarkable things."

Trust opens up new and unimagined possibilities.

Robert C. Solomon

6

Strategies for Leaders to Strengthen Connection

Strengthening the connection between leaders and employees is essential for fostering a positive and productive work environment. When leaders prioritize building strong relationships with their team members, they create a culture of trust, engagement, and collaboration. This connection not only enhances individual performance but also drives organizational success. Here's a detailed overview of how leaders can strengthen employee connections and the benefits of doing so.

Open and Transparent Communication

Effective communication is the foundation of strong employee connections. Leaders should prioritize clear and honest communication, sharing information about organizational goals, changes, and challenges. This transparency builds trust and ensures that employees feel informed and valued. Regular updates and open forums for questions and feedback can reinforce this transparency.

Exercise 1
Weekly Team Updates

- Schedule a weekly team meeting where you provide updates on organizational goals, changes, and challenges.

- Encourage team members to ask questions and share their thoughts.

- Use this time to address any concerns and provide clarity on critical issues.

Active Listening

Active listening involves giving your full attention to employees, reflecting on what is being said, and responding thoughtfully. This approach shows employees that their opinions and contributions matter, fostering a sense of belonging and commitment.

Exercise 2
One-on-One Meetings

- Schedule regular one-on-one meetings with each team member.

- During these meetings, practice active listening by focusing on the speaker without distractions.

- Summarize what the employee has said and respond thoughtfully, ensuring they feel heard and valued.

Empathy and Understanding

Demonstrating empathy involves understanding and sharing the feelings of others. Leaders who practice empathy can better recognize employee needs and build trust. Being attuned to employees' feelings and needs allows leaders to respond appropriately and supportively.

Exercise 3
Empathy Mapping

- Create an empathy map for each team member, outlining their feelings, needs, and challenges.

- Use this map to guide your interactions and support efforts.

- Regularly update the empathy map based on new insights and feedback from team members.

Recognition and Appreciation

Regularly acknowledging and celebrating employee achievements reinforces their sense of value and motivation. Leaders should provide constructive feedback and recognize both individual and team accomplishments, creating a positive and supportive work environment.

Exercise 4
Recognition Rituals

- Implement a recognition ritual, such as a monthly awards ceremony or a weekly shout-out session.

- Encourage team members to nominate their peers for recognition.

- Celebrate both small and significant achievements to foster a culture of appreciation.

Exercise 5
Professional Development Opportunities

Investing in employees' growth and development shows that leaders are committed to their success. Providing training, mentorship, and career advancement opportunities helps employees feel supported and valued, leading to higher engagement and retention.

Development Plans

- Work with each team member to create a personalized development plan.
- Identify areas for growth and set specific, achievable goals.
- Provide resources and support to help employees achieve their development goals.

By implementing these strategies, leaders can create a more connected and cohesive team:

Benefits of Strengthening Employee Connection

1. ***Building Trust and Credibility:*** Trust is the foundation of strong employee connections. Leaders can build

trust by demonstrating integrity, reliability, and consistency in their actions. Being transparent, keeping promises, and showing respect for employees' contributions are key to establishing and maintaining trust.

2. ***Encouraging Collaboration and Teamwork:*** Fostering a collaborative environment where employees work together towards common goals strengthens connections within the team. Leaders should encourage open communication, teamwork, and the sharing of ideas to create a cohesive and supportive work culture.

3. ***Increased Productivity:*** Employees who feel connected to their peers and leaders are more likely to be engaged in their work, leading to increased productivity and better performance. This engagement stems from a sense of belonging and purpose, which drives employees to go beyond in their roles.

4. ***Enhanced Collaboration:*** Strong connections facilitate open communication and collaboration, enabling

teams to work more effectively toward common goals. When employees trust and respect each other, they are more willing to share knowledge, support one another, and work together to solve problems.

5. ***Improved Employee Retention:*** Organizations that prioritize employee connection often experience lower turnover rates. This is because connected employees feel valued and appreciated, reducing the likelihood of them seeking opportunities elsewhere. Lower turnover rates save costs associated with hiring and training new employees and contribute to a more stable and experienced workforce.

6. ***Greater Innovation:*** A connected workforce is more likely to share ideas and take risks, fostering an environment of creativity and innovation. When employees feel safe and supported, they are more willing to experiment and propose innovative solutions, driving the organization forward.

7. ***Positive Workplace Culture:*** Leadership that promotes connection contributes to a positive organizational culture, making the workplace more enjoyable and

fulfilling. A culture of connection is characterized by mutual respect, inclusiveness, and a shared commitment to the organization's values and goals.

8. ***Supporting Change and Adaptability:*** In today's fast-paced and ever-changing business landscape, effective communication is crucial for supporting change and adaptability. Leaders who communicate clearly about changes, the reasons behind them, and the expected outcomes help employees understand and embrace new initiatives. This transparency reduces resistance to change and fosters a culture of adaptability, where employees are more willing to take on new challenges and contribute to the organization's success.

Summary

The essence of effective leadership lies not just in directing teams, but in forging genuine connections that inspire trust, collaboration, and growth. Leaders who prioritize open communication, active listening, and authentic engagement foster environments where individuals feel valued and empowered. By consistently nurturing relationships, providing clear vision, and offering encouragement, leaders bridge gaps between themselves and their teams, cultivating loyalty and motivation. Ultimately, the most impactful strategies for strengthening the leader connection revolve around sincerity, empathy, and a steadfast commitment to collective success. When leaders embrace these principles, they not only enhance their own influence, but also unlock the full potential of those they lead.

7

Challenges and Barriers

Leadership connection faces several challenges in the workplace, particularly when dealing with generational differences and the evolving landscape of remote work settings. These challenges can influence how teams communicate, function, and grow, ultimately shaping the overall organizational culture and determining the success of collaborative initiatives.

Generational differences often present distinct challenges and barriers that can impact communication and collaboration within teams. Here's a breakdown of some of the challenges across generations like Millennials (Gen Y), Gen X, and Gen Z:

- *__Communication Styles:__* Millennials and Gen Z tend to prefer digital communication methods such as emails, instant messaging, and collaboration tools, while Gen X may lean more towards face-to-face or phone conversations. This difference can lead to misunderstandings or feelings of exclusion. Additionally, the informal tone favored by younger generations in communication can sometimes be seen as unprofessional by older colleagues.

- ***Technological Adaptation:*** Millennials and Gen Z are more tech-savvy and adaptive to recent technologies. In contrast, Gen X may take longer to adapt or feel less comfortable with constant technological change. The rapid pace of digital transformation can create skill gaps between generations, making it challenging for teams to work cohesively without additional training.

- ***Feedback and Leadership Styles:*** Millennials and Gen Z typically desire regular feedback, mentoring, and a collaborative work environment. They often expect leaders to be approachable and transparent. Gen X may be more independent and prefer less oversight, seeing regular feedback as micromanagement. This difference in expectations can create tension between leadership styles.

- ***Career Development and Mobility:*** Millennials and Gen Z tend to view jobs as steppingstones and are more likely to switch roles for better opportunities, career growth, or alignment with personal values. Gen X, having experienced economic volatility, may value loyalty and long-term employment more, which can lead to tension in teams where younger colleagues are seen as less committed.

- ***Perceptions of Authority:*** Younger generations, particularly Gen Z, may question traditional authority and be more vocal about organizational practices, equality, and fairness. Gen X, having been in the workforce longer, may place more trust in the system or hierarchy, potentially creating friction in environments that emphasize collaborative or decentralized decision-making.

- ***Attitudes Toward Diversity and Inclusion:*** Gen Z and Millennials are typically more attuned to issues related to diversity, equity, and inclusion. They may challenge outdated policies or call for more active social responsibility from companies. Gen X may have different perspectives on these issues, based on the workplace cultures they've been a part of, viewing certain diversity initiatives as disruptive or unnecessary.

- ***Workplace Expectations:*** Millennials and Gen Z often prioritize work-life balance, flexibility, and purpose-driven work. They may expect remote work options and flexible hours, which can be at odds with Gen X's traditional 9-to-5 mindset. Gen X values job stability and autonomy but may not fully understand the younger generation's demand for instant feedback and rapid career progression.

Understanding and addressing these generational and environmental challenges is crucial for leaders aiming to build meaningful connections with their teams. Adapting communication styles, management approaches, and organizational policies to be inclusive of all generations can pave the way for increased collaboration, innovation, and long-term organizational success.

Remote Work Settings

The shift toward remote and hybrid work models has transformed how businesses operate, particularly due to COVID-19 and the economic challenges faced by brick-and-mortar establishments. Remote work settings present unique challenges and barriers that can impact leadership connection:

1. ***Communication Gaps:*** Remote work can lead to communication gaps, as digital communication tools may lack the emotional nuance of in-person conversations. This can make it harder for leaders to connect authentically with their teams.

2. ***Feelings of Isolation:*** Employees working remotely may experience feelings of isolation or disconnect from the team. This can affect morale and productivity, as employees may feel less engaged and supported.

3. ***Maintaining Work-Life Boundaries:*** Remote work can blur the lines between personal and professional life, making it difficult for employees to maintain work-

life boundaries. Leaders must be mindful of this and provide support to help employees manage their responsibilities.

4. ___Technological Challenges:___ Remote work requires reliable technology and internet access. Leaders must ensure that employees have the necessary tools and resources to work effectively from home.

5. ___Geographical Separation:___ Physical separation makes it harder for leaders to build personal connections with their teams. Remote work settings require leaders to find new ways to foster connection and collaboration.

6. **Managing Hybrid Teams:** Hybrid work models, where employees split their time between working remotely and in the office, present challenges in managing schedules and ensuring fair distribution of in-office and remote days. Leaders must ensure that all team members feel included and aligned.

Overcoming These Barriers

To overcome these barriers, leaders can implement several strategies:

1. *Intergenerational Training Programs:* Promote understanding and empathy through training programs that bridge communication and cultural gaps between generations.

2. *Flexible Workplace Policies:* Cater to the diverse needs of different generations with hybrid work models, mentorship programs, and flexible hours.

3. *Promoting Continuous Learning:* Invest in technological upskilling to alleviate the generational divide regarding tech adoption.

4. *Inclusive Leadership:* Value and incorporate input from all generations to ensure equitable workplace dynamics.

By acknowledging and addressing these challenges and barriers, leaders can foster a more cohesive and productive workforce, creating a positive and engaging work environment. Recognizing generational differences and fostering environments that respect each group's unique strengths, companies can mitigate barriers and create a more cohesive and productive workforce.

The Re-start

Restarting the connection with a team as a leader is sometimes, especially after being in a position for some time, crucial for maintaining morale, productivity, and a sense of cohesion.

Here's a detailed approach to effectively reconnecting with the team:

1. **Self-Reflection**

   - *Evaluate Leadership Style:* Reflect on your leadership approach, communication, and interaction with the team. Identify areas where you may have become disconnected.

   - *Acknowledge Changes:* Recognize any changes within the team dynamics, goals, or individual roles that may have influenced the relationship.

- *__Schedule One-on-One Meetings:__* Engage in individual conversations to understand team members' perspectives, concerns, and suggestions. This fosters trust and shows that you value their input.

- *__Conduct Team Meetings:__* Organize a team meeting to openly discuss the importance of reconnecting. Encourage team members to share their thoughts and feelings about team dynamics and project goals.

2. *__Reestablish Trust__*

   - *Be Transparent:* Share your thoughts on the current state of the team and the direction you wish to take. Transparency builds trust and encourages honesty.

   - *Admit Mistakes:* If there have been missteps or decisions that affected the team negatively, acknowledge them openly. This shows vulnerability and willingness to improve.

3. **_Create Opportunities for Engagement_**

- *Team-building Activities:* Organize informal gatherings or team-building exercises to strengthen relationships outside of work tasks. This can help ease tensions and foster camaraderie.

- *Collaborative Projects:* Introduce initiatives that require team collaboration, emphasizing the importance of each member's contribution. This reinforces a sense of unity and purpose.

4. **_Revisit and Realign Goals_**

- *Set New Goals Together:* Involve the team in redefining goals and objectives, ensuring that everyone has a say in the direction of the team. This can reignite motivation and ownership of tasks.

- *Regular Check-ins:* Implement a system for regular progress check-ins to ensure everyone feels aligned and supported. This reinforces accountability and connection.

5. _Foster a Supportive Environment_

- *Encourage Feedback:* Create a culture where feedback is welcomed and acted upon. Regularly solicit input on your leadership style and team processes to promote continuous improvement.

- *Recognize Contributions:* Acknowledge individual and team achievements publicly. Celebrating success helps build morale and reinforces a positive team culture.

6. . _Model the Behavior You Want to See -_

- *Be Approachable:* Maintain an open-door policy and be available to your team. This encourages team members to come forward with concerns or ideas.

- *Exhibit Empathy:* Show understanding and support for personal and professional challenges team members may face. Empathy strengthens bonds and fosters loyalty.

7. **_Monitor Progress and Adjust_**

- *Evaluate Team Dynamics:* Continuously assess the atmosphere within the team and your connection with team members. Be ready to adapt your approach, as necessary.

- *Solicit Ongoing Feedback:* Make it a habit to ask for feedback on team interactions and your leadership. This demonstrates commitment to growth and fosters a culture of improvement.

Earlier in my career, I sometimes struggled to connect with teams after changing roles. Effective reconnection requires being intentional, humble, and open to ongoing dialogue. Using these strategies helps leaders build motivated, goal-aligned teams where everyone feels valued.

If your actions inspire others to dream more, learn more, do more and become more, you are a leader.

John Quincy Adams

—————))•((—————

8

Managing Various Size Teams

Managing small, medium, and large teams requires different approaches due to variations in team dynamics, communication needs, leadership strategies, and operational complexity.

1. *__Managing Small Teams__*
   (up to 10 people):

   - *Communication:* Direct and personal. Regular one-on-one interactions are common, and team members can have direct access to the manager.

   - *Decision-Making:* Quick, often informal, and usually involves the whole team in discussions. Consensus-building is easier.

   - *Team Dynamics:* Easier to build close relationships and trust. Conflicts are often addressed quickly due to the intimate setting.

- *Management Style:* More hands-on, with a focus on coaching and mentorship. The manager may collaborate closely with the team.

- *Flexibility:* Easier to be agile and adapt to changes quickly.

2. **Managing Medium Teams**

(10-50 people):

- *Communication:* Requires more structure, like regular team meetings or group updates. The manager may rely on team leaders or department heads for communication.

- *Decision-Making:* More formal, often with input from subgroups or leaders within the team. It may take longer to reach decisions compared to small teams.

- *Team Dynamics:* Relationship building becomes more complex, and subgroups or cliques may form. Managing these dynamics becomes important to maintain team cohesion.

- *Management Style:* Managers may delegate more tasks and focus on strategic decisions rather than day-to-day tasks.

- *Systems & Processes:* Clear processes and defined roles are necessary to ensure coordination across the team.

3. _**Managing Large Teams**_
   (50+ people):

- *Communication:* More hierarchical, often using layers of management or departmental heads. Communication tools (e.g., newsletters, communication platforms) are essential to keep everyone informed.

- *Decision-Making:* Requires formal processes with multiple layers of approval or input. Decision-making is becoming slower due to the need for consensus across departments.

- *Team Dynamics:* Team culture and morale are influenced by sub-leaders, and managing cross-team relationships is crucial. It's harder to maintain a personal connection with everyone.

- *Management Style:* High reliance on delegation. The manager focuses on setting high-level goals, strategy, and leadership through middle management.

- *Systems & Structure:* Detailed processes, robust systems, and clear reporting structures are needed to maintain efficiency and control.

Each size demands different skills from the manager. While small teams benefit from personal leadership and flexibility, large teams require strategic oversight, delegation, and structured management.

Managing larger teams requires a balance of strong leadership, communication, and strategic planning. Here are some strategies to help you effectively manage larger teams:

Clear Communication Channels

- *Establish Structure:* With larger teams, it's important to create clear lines of communication and designate specific channels for diverse types of information.

- *Frequent Updates:* Use team meetings, emails, and project management tools to ensure everyone stays informed.

Delegate Effectively

- *Empower Leaders:* Break the team into smaller groups, each led by a trusted team leader or supervisor.

- *Trust in Delegation:* Clearly define responsibilities for each group, empowering them to make decisions within their area.

Set Clear Expectations

- *Define Roles:* Make sure every team member understands their role and the team's overall objectives.

- *SMART Goals:* Implement Specific, Measurable, Achievable, Relevant, and Time-bound goals for clarity and accountability.

Utilize Technology

- Team Collaboration Tools: Platforms like Slack, Microsoft Teams, or Trello can improve collaboration and make managing tasks easier.

- Tracking and Reporting: Use dashboards to track performance, progress, and KPIs (Key Performance Indicators)

Foster Team Morale and Culture

- Engage Employees: Regularly recognize achievements and contributions. Keep morale high with team-building activities.
- Encourage Feedback: Implement a system where team members can share their thoughts, both informally and formally.

Prioritize Time Management

- Plan: With more people, there will be more moving parts, so effective planning is critical.

- Efficient Meetings: Keep meetings brief and focused, making sure agendas are set.

9

Overcoming Bias and Cultural Differences

In today's globalized society, interactions among diverse cultures are common in every aspect of life. While diversity enables growth and innovation, it also brings challenges like bias and cultural misunderstandings. Addressing these issues is essential for building inclusive and successful communities and organizations.

Bias is an unfair inclination or prejudice, either conscious or unconscious, that affects our attitudes and actions. Cultural differences include the varied beliefs, values, customs, and communication styles across groups.

Overcoming bias and embracing diversity require self-awareness and reflection. Unchecked, bias can perpetuate stereotypes and inequality; managed thoughtfully, diversity fosters creativity and enriches everyone involved.

The Roots and Impact of Bias

Bias is a natural part of human cognition. Our brains are wired to categorize information rapidly, an evolutionary trait that once helped our ancestors survive. However, in the modern world, these mental shortcuts known as heuristics can lead us astray. Implicit biases operate below the level of conscious awareness, influencing our judgments even when we believe ourselves to be fair-minded.

The impact of bias is far-reaching. In the workplace, bias can affect hiring, promotions, and team dynamics, leading to a lack of diversity and missed opportunities for innovation. In education, biased expectations can influence student performance and self-esteem. On a societal level, bias perpetuates discrimination, social divisions, and systemic injustice.

Navigating Cultural Differences

Culture shapes our worldviews and informs our sense of what is "normal" or appropriate. When people from different cultures interact, differences in communication styles, attitudes toward authority, concepts of time, and approaches to conflict can lead to confusion and frustration. Misunderstandings may arise not out of malice but from differing frames of reference.

For example, in some cultures, direct eye contact is a sign of confidence and honesty, while in others it may be seen as disrespectful or confrontational. Similarly, notions of personal space, punctuality, and formality vary widely across societies. Recognizing these differences and approaching them with curiosity rather than judgment is essential to building meaningful cross-cultural relationships.

Strategies for Overcoming Bias

1. *Self-Reflection and Education:* The journey to overcoming bias begins with introspection. Individuals must be willing to question their assumptions and acknowledge their own blind spots. Participating in workshops, reading diverse perspectives, and seeking out cultural education are valuable first steps.

2. ***Implicit Bias Training:*** Many organizations now offer training designed to help employees recognize and mitigate unconscious bias. While not a complete solution, such programs can raise awareness and initiate difficult but necessary conversations.

3. ***Perspective-Taking:*** Empathy is a powerful antidote to bias. By consciously adopting the perspective of others, we begin to understand their experiences, motivations, and frustrations. This can be practiced through storytelling, dialogue, and cultural immersion.

4. ***Accountability and Allyship:*** Overcoming bias is not solely an individual endeavor. Organizations and communities must put systems in place to ensure fairness in decision-making. This includes transparent policies, diverse leadership, and mechanisms for addressing grievances. Allies those who use their privilege to advocate for others play a crucial role in dismantling systemic bias.

Bridging Cultural Differences

- *Developing Cultural Intelligence:* Cultural intelligence (CQ) refers to the ability to relate and work effectively across cultures. It involves cognitive, motivational, and behavioral competencies that allow individuals to adapt to new cultural contexts. Building CQ requires openness, flexibility, and a willingness to learn from mistakes.

- *Effective Communication:* Clear, respectful communication is the foundation of successful cross-cultural interaction. This includes active listening, avoiding assumptions, and being mindful of nonverbal cues. When misunderstandings occur, they should be seen as opportunities for learning rather than sources of blame.

- *Celebrating Diversity:* Creating spaces where cultural differences are not merely tolerated but celebrated encourages a sense of belonging for all. This can be achieved through multicultural events, inclusive curriculum, and the acknowledgement of diverse holidays and traditions.

■ *Collaborative Problem-Solving:* Diverse teams often approach challenges from multiple angles, resulting in more creative solutions. Fostering collaboration across cultures requires patience, trust, and a recognition that different approaches can be equally valid and effective.

Case Studies and Examples

Consider multinational companies that have succeeded by embracing diversity—such as Google's global teams, which harness the strengths of employees from every corner of the world. Alternatively, look at educational institutions that have implemented inclusive teaching strategies, resulting in higher engagement and achievement among students from different backgrounds. On an individual level, travelers who immerse themselves in new cultures often discover a deeper appreciation for both the differences and the commonalities that unite us.

Overcoming Challenges

The journey toward overcoming bias and bridging cultural gaps is not without obstacles. Resistance to change, entrenched power structures, and the temptation to retreat into familiar circles can impede progress. However, each challenge also represents an opportunity for growth. By persevering in the face of discomfort and uncertainty, individuals and organizations can develop resilience and adaptability.

The Role of Leadership

Leaders set the tone for inclusive and cross-cultural understanding. By modeling openness, humility, and a commitment to continuous learning, leaders can inspire others to follow suit. They must also be willing to confront bias and inequity wherever they appear, ensuring that policies and practices reflect the values of fairness and respect.

The Personal Journey

Ultimately, overcoming bias and embracing cultural differences is a personal as well as a collective endeavor. It requires humility, the recognition that no one has all the answers and a willingness to grow. It demands courage to confront uncomfortable truths and the grace to forgive oneself and others for mistakes along the way.

Conclusion

Reflecting on my journey, I realize how transformative it has been to embrace differences and to become a catalyst for positive cultural change within my teams. The work of overcoming bias and truly valuing diverse perspectives is ongoing—it never really ends. But that's what makes it so powerful and essential, especially in a business context. Every day, by making the conscious choice to foster inclusion, we not only grow as individuals but also strengthen our teams, drive innovation, and create environments where people genuinely want to contribute their best.

In the workplace, our commitment to continuous improvement—to keep learning from each other another, revisiting our assumptions, and building deeper connections—makes us all better. It isn't just about meeting metrics or crossing items off a list; it's about shaping a culture where everyone feels empowered and valued, and where success is built on collaboration and mutual respect.

Ultimately, the legacy we build in our professional lives isn't measured by the barriers we maintain, but by the bridges we create and the thriving communities we nurture. By working and growing together, we not only achieve our goals but also cultivate a business environment that's dynamic, resilient, and truly rewarding for everyone involved. Let's keep moving forward, side by side, committed to the kind of progress that lifts us all.

10

Real World Examples

One of the most effective methods for fostering meaningful and lasting learning is the integration of real-world examples into educational experiences. When abstract concepts are grounded in tangible, relatable scenarios drawn from everyday life, learners are more likely to grasp, retain, and apply new knowledge. This approach bridges the gap between theory and practice, connecting curriculum with the complex, nuanced reality students will encounter outside the classroom.

Real-World Leaders Fostering Employee Connection

In the realm of leadership, fostering strong employee connections is paramount for driving engagement, productivity, and organizational success. Numerous leaders across various industries have exemplified this principle, demonstrating how effective leadership can transform the workplace culture and enhance employee satisfaction. Here are some notable examples:

Examples

Listening Tour

When Alan Mulally became CEO of Ford in 2006, he started by conducting a "listening tour" across the company. He met with employees at all levels to understand their challenges, ideas, and perspectives. Mulally was known for fostering a culture of open communication by asking simple questions and showing a genuine interest in employees' views. You could implement a similar approach by scheduling time with different departments to listen and learn, focusing on their concerns and how you can support them.

One-on-One Meetings

Many successful leaders, like Satya Nadella, CEO of Microsoft, are renowned for his empathetic leadership style and focus on employee connection. Upon taking the helm in 2014, Nadella prioritized creating a culture of inclusivity and collaboration. He implemented regular one-on-one meetings with direct reports to understand their strengths and align priorities. Nadella's emphasis on open communication and transparency has fostered a sense of trust and belonging among employees, contributing to Microsoft's resurgence as a leading tech company.

Walking the Floor

Howard Schultz, when he returned as Starbucks CEO, would often visit unannounced stores and spend time with baristas. He felt it was important to understand the day-to-day operations and challenges firsthand. Walking the floor in your role—whether in housekeeping, food services, or hospital operations—gives you visibility, demonstrates humility, and provides insight into what employee's experience, fostering strong connections from the ground up.

"Ask Me Anything" Sessions

A frequent practice in many tech companies, "Ask Me Anything" (AMA) sessions help new leaders establish transparency and approachability. For example, when Dara Khosrowshahi took over as CEO of Uber, he hosted several open Q&A sessions to address employee concerns and build trust. You could do something similar by hosting open forums for employees to ask questions about your vision, priorities, and leadership approach.

Aligning on Core Values Early

When Greg Adams became CEO of Kaiser Permanente, he quickly reinforced the organization's commitment to its mission of improving health outcomes. As a new leader in healthcare, emphasizing the shared values of service, compassion, and operational excellence can help rally the team around a common purpose. Early team meetings or leadership huddles could focus on reaffirming these values and discussing how each department can embody them.

Quick Wins to Build Trust

In many leadership transitions, focusing on early wins is key to gaining credibility. Mary Barra, GM's CEO, concentrated on critical but attainable changes early in her leadership to show quick results. In your case, focusing on resolving a longstanding operational issue (e.g., improving supply chain processes or addressing employee concerns) can help build trust and show employees that you're committed to making a positive impact quickly.

By implementing these strategies, leaders can create a more connected, motivated, and high-performing workforce.

Overview of Exercises to Build Connection and Engagement

It is essential to reflect on the key insights and strategies we've explored for building strong connections and engagement within a team. These foundational principles are crucial for fostering a positive and productive work environment, aligning everyone with the organization's mission and core values.

Throughout these chapters, we've delved into the importance of effective communication, emotional intelligence, inclusivity, and understanding generational differences. We've also examined the impact of various leadership styles on employee connection and engagement. By understanding and implementing these strategies and insights, leaders can create a more connected and engaged workforce, driving organizational success. As we move forward, let's continue to build on these principles and explore new ways to strengthen the connection between leaders and employees.

Team Meeting

Regular team meetings are a fantastic way to review expectations, goals, and direction. Start with an honest, open conversation and a dose of transparency. Discuss how you can accomplish goals together. For example, ask, "How can we accomplish this _____?" and be transparent by saying, "I'm not sure, but here are some ideas or let's plan strategy sessions."

Employee Connect

Focus on building a rapport with your team members. Take the time to listen to their thoughts and concerns. Schedule individual meetings to establish personal connections. Spend time in different areas to understand the day-to-day operations. Organize meetings with members from different departments to foster collaboration.

"Ask Me Anything" Sessions

Host open forums where team members can ask questions and share their thoughts. These sessions create opportunities for engagement and connection among participants, allowing them to feel part of a community. Encourage real-time interaction and immediate responses to foster a dynamic and engaging atmosphere.

Aligning on Core Values Early

Discuss and align the core values that will guide your team. Start with a team meeting to review expectations, goals, and direction. Have an honest, open conversation about core values and how they will guide the team. This helps create a cohesive organizational culture, fostering a sense of belonging and purpose among employees.

Quick Wins to Build Trust

Identify and achieve quick wins to build trust and demonstrate your commitment. Communicate these successes to the team to show that their feedback is valued and acted upon. This approach helps build credibility and fosters a positive work environment.

Conducting a Listening Tour

Define the purpose of the listening tour. Are you seeking to understand employee concerns, gather feedback on recent changes, or develop new strategies? Schedule meetings with various stakeholders, including employees, customers, community members, or other relevant parties. Spend time in different areas of the organization, observe operations, interact with employees, and gather insights on their experiences and challenges.

Walking the Floor

Spend time in different areas of the organization regularly. Observe operations, interact with employees, and gather insights on their experiences and challenges. Ask open-ended questions to encourage employees to share their thoughts and concerns. Take notes on key observations and feedback.

Engaging with Employees

Build personal connections and demonstrate genuine interest in employees' work. Show appreciation for employees' efforts and contributions. Listen actively to employees' feedback and concerns. Provide immediate support or follow up on issues raised during your visit.

Reflecting on Observations

Analyze the insights gathered during your walks and identify areas for improvement. Review your notes and categorize feedback into themes. Identify familiar challenges and areas where employees need support. Develop action plans to address the issues raised.

Implementing Changes

Demonstrate commitment to improving the workplace based on employee feedback. Communicate the changes you plan to implement for the team. Involve employees in the process of making improvements. Monitor the impact of the changes and adjust as needed.

As you embrace and integrate several of these suggested ways to connect, you will not only notice improvements in communication but also foster a deeper sense of collaboration and trust within your team or community. Our consistency in these practices is key—it demonstrates our commitment to building strong, reliable relationships where every individual feels heard and valued.

Implementing these strategies might involve regular check-ins, open channels for feedback, or dedicated time to understanding others' perspectives. Consistency in reaching out, sharing updates, and inviting participation helps create an environment where dialogue is ongoing rather than occasional. Remember, connection is a two-way process: as much as we initiate, we must also actively listen and respond with empathy and respect.

I sincerely encourage you to provide feedback on these methods as you try them out. Let me know what works well, what feels challenging, and how best refine our approach to meet everyone's needs more effectively. Your insights are invaluable in helping tailor these practices to fit this unique context.

Ultimately, sustaining meaningful connections requires ongoing effort, open-mindedness, and the willingness to adapt. By making connections a priority and inviting feedback, we pave the way for growth, innovation, and a more supportive and understanding environment for everyone involved.

Conclusion

I can wholeheartedly attest to these real-world examples—these are not just theories, but living practices I've embraced for years, constantly refining and recommitting to them. The truth is, many leaders overlook these simple but powerful actions, or fail to fully engage with them. Yet, I promise you: when you truly commit, even to just a few of these approaches, you'll witness a remarkable transformation in team engagement and spirit. The change is real, and it's profound. In the next chapter I've outlined some exercises I believe will help you.

11

Reflections & Exercises

By implementing the strategies and insights we have discussed, leaders can create a more connected and engaged workforce, driving organizational success. As we move forward, let's continue to build on these principles and explore new ways to strengthen the connection between leaders and employees.

Types of Meetings to Build Leader-Team Member Connections

1. *Team Meeting:* Building trust and connections in a new leadership team.

2. *Listening Tour:* Take the time to listen to your team members' thoughts and concerns.

3. *One-on-One Meetings:* Schedule individual meetings to establish personal connections.

4.*Walking the Floor:* Spend time in different areas to understand the day-to-day operations.

5. **_Setting Up Cross-Functional Meetings:_** Organize meetings with members from different departments to foster collaboration.

6. **_"Ask Me Anything" Sessions:_** Host open forums where team members can ask questions and share their thoughts.

Key components of these meetings typically include:

- **_Introduction and Background:_** Share your background, leadership style, and vision for the team. Encourage employees to discuss their roles, experiences, and aspirations.

- **_Listening and Feedback:_** Actively listen to employees' thoughts, concerns, and feedback regarding the workplace, team dynamics, and challenges.

- **Goal Setting:** Discuss individual and team goals, aligning personal objectives with the team's or organization's goals.

- **Support and Development:** Identify ways to support employees' development and address their needs for resources, training, or guidance.

- **Establishing Communication Norms:** Set expectations for ongoing communication, including preferences for feedback, check-ins, and future one-on-one meetings.

By engaging in these exercises, you will develop a deeper understanding of how to build trust and connections with your team, setting a solid foundation for your leadership role. These meetings can help create a solid foundation for collaboration, increase employee engagement, and foster a positive workplace culture.

Sample Exercises

Consider a high school biology class studying genetics. Instead of simply memorizing Mendelian laws, students analyze real case studies of inherited diseases, debate ethical considerations of genetic modification, and review news about CRISPR technology. These experiences not only deepen understanding but also ignite curiosity and responsibility.

In business education, reviewing the rise and fall of actual companies through case studies such as Blockbuster, Kodak, or Netflix allows students to examine decision-making, innovation, and adaptation in dynamic markets. These lessons provide invaluable, practical insights that theoretical study alone cannot offer.

Exercise 1

Aligning on Core Values Early

Objective

To establish a unified direction and guiding principles for the team and achieving quick wins to build trust.

Steps

- Start with a team meeting to review expectations, goals, and direction.
- Have an honest, open conversation about core values and how they will guide the team.
- Discuss and align the fundamental beliefs and expectations that will shape the team's culture and decision-making.
- Identify and achieve quick wins that address immediate concerns or operational issues.
- Communicate these successes to the team to show that their feedback is valued and acted upon.

Exercise 2

Hold a Team Meeting

Objective

To explore strategies for building trust and connections with your team as a new leader

Steps

- Schedule a team meeting with your leadership team.

- Review expectations, goals, and direction.

- Start with an honest, open conversation and a dose of transparency.

- Discuss how you can accomplish goals together. For example, ask, "How can we accomplish this _____?" and be transparent by saying, "I'm not sure, but here are some ideas or let's plan strategy sessions."

- Focus on beginning to build a rapport with your team members.

- Discuss and align the core values that will guide your team.

- Identify and achieve quick wins to build trust and demonstrate your commitment.

Exercise 3

Conducting a Listening Tour

Objective: To explore strategies for building trust and connection with your team through a listening tour

- Define the purpose of the listening tour. Are you seeking to understand employee concerns, gather feedback on recent changes, or develop new strategies?
- Schedule meetings with various stakeholders, including employees, customers, community members, or other relevant parties.

Exercise 4

Conduct One-on-One Meetings

Objective

To have focused, personal discussions with individual team members

Steps

- Schedule private conversations with each employee.
- Provide feedback, discuss goals, address concerns, offer guidance, and foster stronger relationships.
- Exchange ideas, clarify expectations, and ensure alignment of tasks and priorities.
- In a healthcare management context, we use these meetings to align department heads, address operational issues, and manage team performance.

Exercise 5

Walking the Floor

Objective

To understand the day-to-day operations and build rapport with employees.

Steps

- Define the purpose of walking the floor. Are you seeking to understand employee concerns, gather feedback on recent changes, or develop new strategies?

- Schedule time to visit different areas of the organization regularly.

Conducting Walks

- Introduce yourself and explain the purpose of your visit.

- Show appreciation for employees' efforts and contributions.

- Listen actively to employees' feedback and concerns.

- Provide immediate support or follow up on issues raised during your visit.

- Spend time in different areas of the organization.

- Observe operations, interact with employees, and gather insights on their experiences and challenges.

- Ask open-ended questions to encourage employees to share their thoughts and concerns.

- Take notes on key observations and feedback.

Exercise 6

Set Up Cross-Functional Meetings

Objective

To foster collaboration and communication across different departments

Steps

- Organize meetings that bring together team members from various departments.
- Define the purpose and goals of the meeting.
- Identify participants and ensure a balance of perspectives and expertise.
- Create an agenda and share it with participants ahead of time.
- Facilitate the meeting, encourage participation, and keep the discussion on track.
- Follow up meeting notes and track the progress of action items.

Reflection

After completing exercises 1 through 6, reflect on the following questions:

- How did the team respond to the initial meeting and interactions?
- What insights did you gain from the listening tour and the one-on-one meetings?
- How did the team respond to the one-on-one meetings and open conversations?
- What insights did you gain from walking the floor and cross-functional meetings?
- What quick wins were you able to achieve, and how did they build trust with your team?
- How did aligning on core values early influence the team's direction and cohesion?
- How did the feedback gathered influence your understanding of the workplace?
- Review your notes and categorize feedback into themes.
- Identify familiar challenges and areas where employees need support.
- Develop action plans to address the issues raised.

Exercise 7

Hosting "Ask Me Anything" Sessions

Objective

To create an open forum for employees to ask questions and share their thoughts

Steps

- Define the purpose of the AMA session. Are you seeking to understand employee concerns, gathering feedback on recent changes, or providing insights on specific topics?

- Schedule the AMA session and choose the format (live chat, online seminar, or social media platform).

- Announce the AMA session to your team, explaining its purpose and encouraging participation.

- Set guidelines for the session, such as the types of questions that can be asked and the expected duration.

- Encourage real-time interaction and immediate responses to foster a dynamic and engaging atmosphere.

- Use these sessions to build transparency and approachability.

Conducting the AMA Session

- Start the session by introducing yourself and explaining the format.
- Encourage participants to ask any questions, ranging from individual experiences to professional insights.
- Provide real-time responses to questions, fostering a dynamic and interactive atmosphere.
- Share your knowledge and experiences, provide unique insights, and build trust with your team.

Engaging with Participants

- Listen actively to each question and respond thoughtfully.
- Show appreciation for employees' participation and contributions.
- Address any concerns or feedback raised during the session.
- Follow up on any questions that require further information or action.

Reflecting on the Session

Objective

To analyze the insights gathered during the AMA session and identify areas for improvement.

- Review the questions and feedback received during the session.
- How did employees respond to the AMA session and your interactions?
- Identify common themes and areas where employees need support.
- Develop action plans to address the issues raised.
- What insights did you gain from the questions and feedback received?
- How did the session impact team collaboration and transparency?
- What changes were you able to implement based on the feedback, and how did they impact the team?
- How did hosting the AMA session help build trust and connections with your team?
- Communicate the outcomes of the session to the team, demonstrating your commitment to improving the workplace based on their feedback.:

Implementing Changes

Objective

To demonstrate commitment to improving the workplace based on employee feedback

Steps

- Communicate the changes you plan to implement for the team.
- Involve employees in the process of making improvements.
- Monitor the impact of the changes and adjust as needed.

Reflection

After completing the exercise, reflect on the following question:

- What changes were you able to implement, and how did they impact the team?

Conclusion

Real-world examples are more than mere illustrations; they are essential bridges between learning and living. When used thoughtfully, they transform education from passive absorption to active construction, equipping learners with not only knowledge but also the wisdom to apply it. For educators and learners alike, seeking connections between the classroom and the world beyond is the key to meaningful, memorable, and impactful learning experiences.

Education is a lifetime knowledge.

Lailah Gifty Akita

———————————— ≫•《 ————————————

12

Conclusion

As I reflect on the journey of building a thriving workplace, I'm reminded that real, lasting change begins with the choices we make as leaders and colleagues every day. Reducing employee turnover isn't just about ticking boxes or implementing generic programs, it's about truly listening to one another, responding with empathy, and being willing to grow together.

In my experience, the most profound transformation happens when we communicate openly with our teams, share our intentions honestly, and invite everyone into the process of making things better. When employees are involved not just as bystanders but as active contributors, there's a renewed sense of belonging and ownership that breathes life into the organization.

I've seen the value of monitoring our progress, asking honest questions, and reflecting on what works and what doesn't.

It's not just about numbers or performance metrics it's about people's real experiences and feelings at work. Adjusting along the way is a sign of strength, not weakness.

A positive workplace culture doesn't emerge overnight. It's cultivated through daily acts of kindness, respect, and recognition, both big and small. When we celebrate each other's achievements and encourage growth, we send a powerful message: you matter here.

Supporting professional growth has always struck me as one of the most meaningful investments we can make. Providing opportunities for learning and advancement shows that we believe in our people's potential and want them to envision a future with us.

Recognition and work-life balance are not mere perks, they're essential. Taking the time to notice, to say thank you, and to offer flexibility acknowledges employees as whole people, not just workers.

Most importantly, I've learned that sincere feedback and open communication channels create a culture of trust. Acting on that feedback, visibly and authentically, proves our commitment to making the workplace better for everyone.

In the end, reducing employee turnover is about building relationships rooted in trust, respect, and shared purpose. When we prioritize these connections, we create the kind of environment where people want to stay, contribute, and grow. That, to me, is not only the heart of good leadership, but also the foundation of enduring organizational success.

A Call to Action

Reducing employee turnover requires a comprehensive approach that focuses on building trust, creating a positive workplace culture, providing growth opportunities, recognizing contributions, fostering work-life balance, and implementing feedback mechanisms. By prioritizing these strategies, leaders can create a supportive and engaging work environment that encourages employees to stay and thrive within the organization in conclusion, the impact and importance of the connection between employees and leaders cannot be overstated. As organizations strive to navigate the complexities of the modern business landscape, prioritizing this relationship is essential for achieving sustainable success. Leaders must recognize their pivotal role in shaping employee experiences and fostering a culture of trust, engagement, and support. By investing in the development of strong leader-employee connections, organizations can unlock the full potential of their workforce, driving innovation, enhancing performance, and cultivating a thriving organizational culture.

References

6 facts about economic inequality in the U.S., Pew Research Center, (February 7, 2020), https://www.pewresearch.org/short-reads/2020/02/07/6-facts-about-economic-inequality-in-the-u-s/

Black Ownership Statistics 2024https://advocacy.sba.gov/2024/02/01/facts-about-small-business-black-ownership-statistics-2024/ and Annual Business Survey Release Provides Data on Minority-Owned, Veteran-Owned and Women-Owned Businesses, U.S. Census Bureau , (January 28, 2021), https://www.census.gov/newsroom/press-releases/2021/annual-business-survey.html

Black Turnout in the 2020 Election, Newport F., (September 25, 2020), GALLUP, https://news.gallup.com/opinion/polling-matters/320903/black-turnout-2020-election.aspx

Civil Rights Data Collection, Department of Education, (2020 – 2021), https://civilrightsdata.ed.gov/profile/us?surveyYear=2020

Civilian unemployment rate, U.S. Bureau of Statistics (2023), Published (September 10, 2024), https://www.bls.gov/charts/employment-situation/civilian-unemployment-rate.htm

High School Graduation Rates, National Center for Education Statistics (NCES), (May 2024), https://nces.ed.gov/programs/coe/indicator/coi/high-school-graduation-rates

Income Inequality by Country 2025, World Population Review, (2022), Retrieved July, 2025 https://worldpopulationreview.com/country-rankings/income-inequality-by-country

Racism, Discrimination, and Health (June 6- August 14, 2023), KFF Survey, Retrieved January 15, 2025 from, https://www.kff.org/racial-equity-and-health-policy/issue-brief/racial-and-ethnic-disparities-in-mental-health-care-findings-from-the-kff-survey-of-racism-discrimination-and-health/

Racial/Ethnic Disparities in Pregnancy-Related Deaths — United States, 2007–2016, Centers for Disease Control and Prevention (CDC), (September 6, 2019, https://www.cdc.gov/mmwr/volumes/68/wr/mm6835a3.htm

Unemployment rates remained low through the third quarter of 2023 though labor market disparities persist, Moore K., Economic Policy Institute, (2023 Q3), https://www.epi.org/indicators/state-unemployment-race-ethnicity-2023-q3/

Views of Race, Policing and Black Lives Matter in the 5 Years Since George Floyd's Killing. (May 7, 2025) Pew Research Center from 2025. https://www.pewresearch.org/race-and-ethnicity/2025/05/07/views-of-race-policing-and-black-lives-matter-in-the-5-years-since-george-floyds-killing/

Voter turnout rates among black voters in U.S. presidential elections from 1964 to 2020, O'Neil A., (July 4, 2024) https://www.statista.com/statistics/1096577/voter-turnout-black-voters-presidential-elections-historical

Why Supporting Black Owned Businesses Build Wealth, Opportunity, and Stronger Communities, Black Business Lists, (April 26, 2025), https://blackbusinesslists.com/support-black-owned-businesses/

www.ingramcontent.com/pod-product-compliance
Lightning Source LLC
Chambersburg PA
CBHW071241130626
46556CB00003B/1109